W9-AWW-266

Praise for Brian Castner's

THE LONG WALK

"Castner succeeds in taking readers into the mind of a man who is hopelessly scarred by war." —*USA Today*

"Direct and disturbing. . . . A painful but compelling read, even as Castner finds ways to cope, at least partially, with his long walk back at home."
—*Morning Edition* (NPR)

"Brutally honest [and] sharply observed. . . . *The Long Walk* is both harrowing and poignant—an intensely personal story of what it takes not just to survive war, but also to fully leave behind the nightmare of combat and readapt to ordinary life." —*The Daily Beast*

"So viscerally engaging that it's hard to read it without shaking. Castner writes with a keen mind, sharp intellect and literary flair . . . [and] the desperate immediacy of a man whose skin has been burned away."
—*Austin American-Statesman*

"He gives equal, if not more, weight to the time and effort that goes into readjusting to his family life, and his straightforward, unself-conscious writing paints an absorbing picture of war in the twenty-first century. . . . Castner's experience isn't everyone's, of course, but a memoir like his can help to bridge that gap between civilians and today's military." —*NewYorker.com*

"A raw, wrenching, blood-soaked chronicle of the human cost of war. Castner's memoir brings to mind Erich Maria Remarque's masterpiece *All Quiet on the Western Front*."
                                    —Jon Krakauer, author of
                                    Where Men Win Glory

"A powerful book about the long cost of combat and the brotherhood of men at arms. . . . [Castner's] honesty is refreshing and the book is written with such candor and openness that one can't help but root for him."
                    —Anthony Swofford, author of *Jarhead*

"Do you want to know a little something about our war in Iraq? Begin with *The Long Walk*, Brian Castner's elegant, superbly written story about the bomb disposal guys. . . . Here is the reality of the exhausted mind, and of profound thought wandering all Creation: this is what I saw, this is what I did, this is what I have become."
                —Larry Heinemann, author of the National Book
                    Award–winning *Paco's Story* and *Close Quarters*

BRIAN CASTNER

THE LONG WALK

Brian Castner, a graduate of Marquette University with an electrical engineering degree, served three tours in the Middle East as an officer of the U.S. Air Force—two of them as the head of an EOD unit in Iraq. In 2006, he received a Bronze Star for his service. Upon returning to the United States following his service, he consulted as an independent civilian contractor, training military EOD units on tactical bomb-disposal procedures prior to their deployment to Iraq and Afghanistan. He lives in Buffalo, New York, with his wife and children.

briancastner.com

THE LONG WALK

The
LONG
WALK

A Story of War and the
Life That Follows

BRIAN CASTNER

ANCHOR BOOKS
A Division of Random House, Inc.
New York

FIRST ANCHOR BOOKS EDITION, APRIL 2013

The Library of Congress has cataloged the Doubleday edition as follows:
Castner, Brian.
The long walk: a story of war and
the life that follows / Brian Castner.—1st ed.
p. cm.
1. Castner, Brian.
2. Iraq War, 2003—Personal narratives, American.
3. Ordnance disposal units—Iraq.
4. Ordnance disposal units—United States.
5. Iraq War, 2003—Veterans—United States—Biography.
6. United States Air Force—Officers—Biography. I. Title.
DS79.766.C37A3 2013
956.7044'3—dc23   2011052419

Anchor ISBN: 978-0-307-95087-1

Author photograph © Joey Campagna
Book design by Michael Collica

www.anchorbooks.com

Printed in the United States of America
10   9   8

To Jessie, who loves me in spite of all this.

"Then I heard the voice of the Lord saying: Who should I send? Who will go for Us? I said: Here I am. Send me. Then I said: Until when, Lord? And He replied: Until cities lie in ruins without inhabitants, houses are without people, the land is ruined and desolate."

—Isaiah 6:8, 11

"[Providence] became a personality and a dominant force in a world of our own . . . 'Luck'—there was no such thing, for luck comes to man whose foresight and planning can ensure perfection to the highest degree possible, and after that, what cannot be planned or foreseen is in the hands of [Providence]. This was Shackleton's creed."

—Journal entry of Dr. Eric Stewart Marshall, polar explorer, traveling with Ernest Shackleton to the South Pole in 1908

"Life consists in what a man is thinking of all day."

—Ralph Waldo Emerson

Contents

Author's Note

I served as an officer in the United States Air Force from December 1999 to September 2007. I deployed to Saudi Arabia in August 2001, to Balad in central Iraq in January 2005, and to Kirkuk in northern Iraq in May 2006. This is the story of those events, and the times that came after.

Everything in this book feels true. It's as correct as a story can be from someone with blast-induced memory lapses. Nothing was changed to create a moral or to ease discomfort. It's as real as I can make it, though reality and objectivity sometimes have little to do with one another.

THE LONG WALK

1 | *Whirl Is King*

THE FIRST THING you should know about me is that I'm Crazy.

I haven't always been. Until that one day, the day I went Crazy, I was fine. Or I thought I was. Not anymore.

My Crazy is a feeling. It's the worst, most intolerable feeling I've ever had. And it never goes away.

When you're Crazy, you make a list of people you have told, the people you have come out to. My list is small. One best friend but not another. Jimbo and John and Greg, but not the other guys on the team. Your wife but not your mother. Those that you think will get it, will understand.

And now I'm telling you. That I'm Crazy, and I don't know why.

The second thing you should know about me is that I don't know how to fix it. Or control it. Or endure from one moment to the next. The Crazy is winning.

So I run.

I run every day, twice a day sometimes, out the front door of my peaceful suburban home, past sticky blast scenes of sewage, and motor oil, and bloody swamps of trash and debris, ankle deep, filling the road, sidewalks, shop and house doorsteps. I run through dust clouds, blown in off the desert or kicked up by the helo rotor wash. I run past the screaming women that never shut up, don't shut up now. I should have made them stop when I had a chance. I run as fast as I can, as long as I can, my feet hitting the pavement in a furious rhythm, along the river near my home.

I run in the hottest part of the day, the full afternoon blaze, the heat of the black asphalt, baking in the summer sun, rising through my shoes and into my feet. I speed up, but the Crazy feeling is still winning. It overwhelms. Sweat pours down my flushed face, in my eyes. Albietz is chalk white skin and brown dried blood from head to toe. Kermit's skin was blue, after they finally found him and put him in his box. Did Jeff have any skin left to show his mother?

I run every day, on the road and along the river stretching to my left, occasionally veiled by low trees swaying in the sunshine and the light breeze off the water. My left knee started aching five miles ago. My teeth are rotting out of my head. My throat closes. My left eye twitches. The detonation rains concrete chunks on my head, splits my ears, dismantles our robot, and peppers the armored truck with molten steel. I reach for my rifle.

I run down the road outside my home, to the drone of Humvee diesel engines and in the purple sunrise over a flat desert. The Crazy in my chest is full to bursting, but the protest of my overworked lungs and heart tamps it down. The Crazy feeling never leaves, but the run makes the rest of the body scream louder, one din to cover another.

The foot sits in the box. Because why not? Where else would you put it? The foot sat in the box.

I run and don't want to stop. The adrenaline has been building all day, and it finally has a release. The boil overflows. Fidgety legs and shaking arms pump and swing. When I stop, the Crazy feeling refloods my swollen heart, lungs, ribs. My eye twitches. I speed up again.

My head swims and swirls. Helicopters and dust fade. I put my rifle down, shrug off my vest. Sweat wipes clean Albietz's hands, and Ricky's head, and Jeff and Kermit, and . . . and? My knee is screaming louder than the women. My ragged breath shakes my chest. I run, and run, and run, and in the Is try to pound out of my head what once Was.

The C-130 landed in Kirkuk just before dark. A couple of Toyota Hilux pickup trucks, driven by our tired predecessors, were there to meet us at the end of a long and exhausting day. Truth is, they would gladly have met us at any time, in the middle of the night even, because our arrival meant they could leave. Leave to go home, to wives and children and sex and alcohol and sleeping in and not getting shot at. The place we had just come from.

You can drive the little stick-shift Hiluxes on the FOB— our walled Forward Operating Base—because no one is trying to kill you there. It's a foreign reminder of home, a normal thing to do every day. Get in a regular truck and drive, on the right side of the road, at a normal speed, with no one trying to shoot you. Simple pleasure.

Bags of gear piled high in the truck beds, we pulled up to the converted hardened aircraft shelter on the west side of the runway, our home base for the rest of our tour. The French-made blast doors of the HAS were cracked open, and the two-foot-thick rounded concrete roof arched three stories overhead.

Inside were the aluminum bunk trailers, the plywood offices and ops desk, a tent or two housing dusty equipment. Our whole operation, under the protective concrete canopy.

As I lay in bed that night, in my new cell—bed, table, trunk, shelf—I stared at the ceiling. I closed my eyes, and I was in my old room in Balad. I opened them in Kirkuk. Closed, and I smelled the diesel fuel off the droning generator, the dead mice caught in our traps, the rotting tent flaps of my fabric-partitioned room in Balad. Open them and it's just the sheet-metal ceiling of my box in Kirkuk.

I'm back. I'm still here. I never left.

It was less than a year and I was back in Iraq. It was less than a minute and I was back in Iraq.

I needed to be back. I would do better this time.

I lie in bed blown up like a balloon, my chest distended and full. The Crazy feeling has filled me to the brim in the darkness of my bedroom, alone next to my sleeping wife. My left arm has gone numb again, left eye twitching as I attempt to close it. The gurgling in my back is growing, first low, then on my upper left side. My heart beats loud, hard, sporadic. I miss a beat. Speed up, catch up. Miss two. A catch-up again. The more I miss the more the Crazy feeling grows. High, full, boiling sea.

I sit up, turn my feet over the side of the bed, and just try to breathe. My lips tingle and my head spins. My wife has found me on the floor before, face to the pine, a divot on my forehead where I hit the dresser corner on the way down. I lie back down to avoid a repeat.

My heart bumps, skips, and gurgles. My jaw aches and I check again for loose teeth. My eye twitches. And again. The

Crazy feeling builds and builds. It never stops, it never ends, there is no relief.

My helium chest is light as a feather. The weight of the ceiling is a granite block pushing my chest into the bed.

What the fuck is happening to me?

The streets got narrower and narrower as we entered the town of Hawija. The broad highway gave way to two-lane main arteries, then narrower neighborhood roads, then one-lane funnels between high courtyard walls. Over a curb and through one tiny gap, and our driving mirrors on each side snapped off clean, our door handles scraping away rock and concrete in the pinch point. Flanks scoured clean, our armored truck now matched the security vehicles to the front and rear.

No one drives through the heart of Hawija unless forced; so much hate packed into such a small space. But with the ring roads blocked by route-clearance teams and security cordons, we plunged into the center, as fast as the Humvees allowed.

Dodging old blast craters, dead dogs, and mountainous garbage piles, we snaked through fortified neighborhoods before hitting the marketplace at the town's center. In the busy market, the number of civilians suddenly swelled, and our convoy started to get bogged down, weaving but stymied by foot and vehicle traffic. Soon the mass of humanity started to press in, and we slowed further.

"Why are we slowing down?" I yelled up to Ackeret, who was behind the wheel.

"There are people in the way, and they won't fucking move!" came the reply.

Slowing is okay. Stopping is not.

I turned in my seat, faced out. I checked my rifle mag, pistol, stretched in my body armor and readjusted it. Right hand went to the rifle, left hand to the truck door handle. We slowed further.

I searched the crowd. Booths and stalls, selling fruit and electronics, lined the sidewalks. The crowds walked and pushed closer and closer the slower our Humvees went. Kids pointed at us through our armored glass windows, yelling then scurrying back down alleyways that emerged every half block. I scanned for threats, but the tent covers of the shop booths, stretched taut to shade the harsh summer sun, blocked my view of rooftops. Shots from higher ground? An RKG-3 anti-tank grenade, tossed from the opening crowd? The Iraqi Army and local police were nowhere to be seen. I readjusted my rifle again, and popped open the dust covers on my optical sight.

But we had not stopped. Not yet.

Men with flat faces of unreadable sternness, walking alongside, began to look into the Humvee windows. Kids moved up, tapped on the door, and then ran off, disappearing into the rabbit warrens. If the attack comes, it will be quick. The crowd, like a school of fish, will suddenly all turn and move away. The sea parts, the attacker rushes in, grenade already in the air. A detonation, a lance through the flimsy armor, a flash through arm, leg, chest, and then the flock closes again, attacker absorbed, and scatters.

We stopped. Ackeret repeatedly hit the steering wheel in frustration.

I looked out, and the enraged beast was now pressed against the side of the Humvee, banging and yelling.

"We need to get moving!" But we didn't. We had ground to a halt in the center of the market.

I gripped the door handle tighter. If we started to get overrun, we needed to disperse the crowd. There was a small gap, less than eighteen inches, between my door and the edge of the mob. I placed my foot on the bottom of the door, and prepared to push. With no top gunner on our Humvee, we'd have to exit and shoot to get a rioting crowd to move back. In one motion, I would throw the two-hundred-pound door open into the throng as hard as I could and rush out. My rifle would come up and forward, barrel end a battering ram directly into the chest of the man closest to me, pulling the trigger as I moved the rifle back to my shoulder. The man in the red-and-white shirt would die first, bullet into chest with no gap between barrel and skin. The next three, teenager in a Nike shirt, older man in a tan man-dress, and another with a bike, would die from my shots two feet away, probably as they fell back in reaction to Red-and-White going down. With the crowd knocked back from the force of the opening door and the shock of the first four dead, I would have time to remount. And if not, if I was swarmed and my rifle grabbed, the pistol in the cross-draw holster on my chest was in easy reach of one hand. It could come out, and need not move far for me to fire and earn me a second or two.

The crowd had to break. The convoy had to move. I would get back to the FOB. I would get home.

I chose who would die in what order. Red-and-White, Nike Shirt, Man-Dress, then Bike. I looked in their eyes, flipped the safety on my rifle to Single, and waited.

I waited for the shot to come. It didn't.

I waited for the grenade to be thrown. It wasn't.

I waited for the mob to riot. They didn't.

With a crawl, we started to move again, and drove off.

The Crazy didn't start right away. It stalked me for years.

Your first sign something may be amiss comes quickly, the moment you get off the plane at the airport in Baltimore. After months of deprivation, American excess is overwhelming. Crowds of self-important bustling businessmen. Shrill and impatient advertising that saturates your eyes and ears. Five choices of restaurant, with a hundred menu items each, only a half-minute walk away at all times. In the land you just left, dinners are uniformly brown and served on trays when served at all. I was disoriented by the choice, the lights, the infinite variety of gummy candy that filled an entire wall of the convenience store, a gluttonous buffet repeated every four gates. The simple pleasure of a cup of coffee after a good night's sleep, sleep you haven't had since you received your deployment orders, seems overly simple when reunited with such a vast volume of overindulgent options.

But the shock wears off, more quickly for some, but eventually for most. Fast food and alcohol are seductive, and I didn't fight too hard. Your old routine is easy to fall back into, preferences and tastes return. It's not hard to be a fussy, overstuffed American. After a couple of months, home is no longer foreign, and you are free to resume your old life.

I thought I did. Resume my old life, that is. I was wrong.

The car bomb went off just outside of our FOB, in downtown Kirkuk, on the highway that leads north to Irbil and the peaceful Kurdish lands untouched by the war. We felt it in the HAS, a shaking rumble like thunder on a clear hot day. We had put our gear on and were waiting for our security escort even before the call came in to go investigate.

The car had stopped burning by the time we arrived. A

twisted black shell, frame, and engine block smoldering, hot to the touch. The Iraqi Police had cordoned off the scene, yelling at pedestrians to move back. The reverse dichotomy always struck me. The scene of the blast, where so much violence had happened minutes before, was now empty and quiet. The surrounding neighborhood, peaceful until the attack, was now a roiling cauldron of frustration and anger.

Castleman and I started the investigation at the blast hole. The asphalt punctured, wet with a mix of fluids, some mechanical, some human. The car frame was several feet from the crater, thrown by the force of the explosion. It yielded no clues; any wires, switches, batteries, or fingerprints were burned away in the fire. We could have found traces of explosive residue if we had had the time. We didn't have the time.

I looked up from the hulk and surveyed further out. Chunks of steel frag were buried in a nearby concrete wall. A fully intact artillery projectile, a 130 or 155, probably, from the size and shape, failing to detonate and instead kicked out by the blast, was caught in a fence a hundred feet away. We would grab that and blow it before we left.

"It smells like shit!" I said. And it did.

"Sir, it always smells like shit in this country," answered Castleman.

He was right. But this wasn't the normal smell of shit: diesel exhaust, burning trash, sweat, and grime, the body odor of an unwashed city. We smelled that mix every day. No, this smelled like actual shit. Human shit.

"Check this out," called Castleman.

He had found the target of the car bomb. Bloody shirts and boots of Iraqi policemen. A pair of pants, dropped or torn off, with a month's wages in frayed and scorched 250-dinar notes poking out from a front pocket. Hands and feet. Several pools of drying blood. The smell of shit was stifling, and getting worse.

A quick count of right hands indicated a couple dead, at least. Who knows how many wounded, pulled out by their fellow police, now dead or dying at the overwhelmed hospital. The Iraqi cops had already picked up the biggest parts, so any count we made was going to be wrong. It wasn't worth the trouble to get the exact right number anyway. I continued on.

The smell of shit was overwhelming in the afternoon heat. I looked down.

"Hey, I found it!" I yelled to Castleman, who was taking pictures of the scene for evidence.

There at my feet was a perfectly formed, and entirely intact, lower intestine. The small intestine above and anus below were torn off and scattered, but the colon itself was pristine, and lay there like I had just removed it from the organ bag in the gut of a Thanksgiving turkey. It was beautiful, stuffed with the digested remains of an unknown last meal.

Castleman walked over and looked down where I pointed. The intestine smelled like it was cooking in a pan.

He shrugged. I shrugged back.

We walked off and left that shit-filled colon to bake on the black asphalt in the hot Iraqi summer sun.

The cigar must have been a Cuban. If not, it was still damn good.

Cubans were readily available in Iraq, and the Colonel, an old fighter pilot, seemed like he knew his cigars. I didn't know where he got them, and I didn't ask. I simply appreciated being offered one, as we sat and talked in the dark hot desert night.

Boom! Ba-boom!

The 155-millimeter howitzers hadn't stopped for the last hour. I only saw the initial flashes when the guns fired and the result where they landed; the dark dusty haze obscured the artillery pieces themselves.

The Colonel and I sat outside our tent, our temporary sleeping quarters for the night, and watched the show. Tiki torches and miniature lights on a string, bulbs encased in brightly colored Easter Island heads, ringed our makeshift smoke pit. I missed a glass of whiskey, but the cigar, warm night, relaxing chair, and conversation took me back to many a patio bar at home.

Boom! Thump thump thump thump!

The guns never paused as chopper after chopper dredged the same route all night. Wounded and dead came home, fresh Marines went out. The landing lights of the birds flicked on once they hit the edge of the air base, Al Taqaddum, a desolate hole up the Euphrates in western Iraq that the Colonel and I were stuck at for the night. Sticky and wet the helos returned, pausing at the pad, unloading their dripping cargo, and then up and turning to reload grunts on the other end of the base. Round and round they went on their grisly circuit.

Boom! Boom boom boom!

Three illumination rounds followed the high explosives into the town of Habbaniyah, a bad neighborhood on the floodplain below us. The illum rounds hung in the air, kept aloft by parachutes as their candles bathed the town in an eerie too-white light, temporary spotlights for the Marines moving house to house. Small-arms fire popped and belt-fed automatic machine guns carried on their conversation in the distance, beneath our high plateau.

We sat and talked because this wasn't our fight. We were just stuck there, waiting on a bird to Baghdad.

A student of history, the Colonel had been telling me stories all night. Stories of the old British Royal Air Force Base in Habbaniyah, a strip of concrete in that very town, now being shelled as we watched. How the Iraqi Army, Axis sympathizers, had surrounded the base in 1941, putting artillery on the bluff where we were now sitting. How the RAF decided to strike first, with old World War I–era biplanes, because they had few ground troops to defend the airfield. The Brits launched the aircraft and banked immediately, right into the teeth of the surprised Iraqis, dropping bombs just hundreds of feet from the base's fence line. They then returned and landed, rearmed and refueled as Iraqi artillery rained on their heads, and launched again, strafing the army on their doorstep. Every sortie was continuously in range of Iraqi anti–aircraft fire, from start to finish. The Brits flew anyway.

The siege lasted four days. By then the pilots had to steer around craters on the runway to take off and land. But they did, and the Brits won. Thirty-three obsolete aircraft turned aside a brigade.

It's a story of British pluck and ingenuity. It's a story of bravado at its height. It's a lullaby old fighter pilots tell their young.

Boom! Thump thump thump! Boom!

We puffed on our cigars, and blew smoke rings, and told war stories, and watched new ones being written, in the glow of the tiki torches and colored lights, until late into the night.

What is the Crazy like? How does it actually feel? Do you remember the last week of school before summer vacation? How it felt as a kid to be almost done for the year, but not quite?

You are sitting at a small desk, bathed in sunlight, by a wall of windows, one open to let in the waning cool breeze. Your armpits begin to moisten in the still classroom air, and a single drop of sweat forms on your forehead as the school starts to heat. Lawn mowers buzz in the distance, and you get the first smell of summer: cut grass on a warm day. It smells like soccer games, catching crawfish in the creek, and dreaming of sneaking off to kiss your middle-school crush behind the big oak tree in the neighborhood park. It smells like playing street hockey with your best friend all day long until his mom calls you inside to stay for dinner. It smells like girls in short shorts and bikini tops. It smells like you've waited nine long months to smell that smell. It smells perfect.

The only thing standing between you and summer is this exam, and there are only three of you left in the classroom. Everyone else is finished and gone, completed their tests for the summer, but you remain as time runs out. The American history exam swims before your eyes. The gulfs of Mexico and Tonkin blend together. How can you take this exam when every atom in your body screams to escape outside into the sunshine? You long to run and play, though you haven't played in years. You take the exam as quickly as possible; the goal becomes to simply finish, and the grade is secondary. Your heart pines for the fresh air, and your chest fills until ready to burst. You have to finish . . . this . . . exam . . . now.

My Crazy is just like that. Except, when you do finally finish the test, hand it in, sprint from the exam room, grab your book bag and run outside . . . there is no relief. There is no relaxation. You feel no different. You're just Crazy in the goddamn sunshine. Every day. All the time.

The cordon was set. The IED was cleared. The security was still in place. The robot was driving back to us, our truck sheltered by the interposed armored vehicles of our infantry fire-team escort, as we packed up our remaining gear and prepared to move. All that remained was picking up the precious pieces.

Uniform concrete apartment buildings loomed over the traffic circle, closed off by our security so we could clear the bomb at its far edge. An empty bowl—with occasional spectators surrounding, staring at every move we made.

The explosive-filled water bottle we deployed had broken apart the bomb's outer shell, but we still needed to pick up the revealed inner workings. Detonating cord and electrical wires held the various pieces of foam casing together in a jumbled mess. A cell phone peeked out of one misshapen lump; PROPHET would want us to snag that so they could rip the SIM card. Every other heavy foam chunk held an EFP, an Explosively Formed Projectile—a steel and copper and explosives mix that punctures armor and splatters molten metal around inside our trucks. We hate them. This one was set up across from the Iraqi Police station. Targeting them? Placed by them? We never do find out.

EFPs are real bad. They take off legs and heads, put holes in armor and engine blocks, and our bosses in Baghdad and Washington want every one we find. So we aren't going to blow these up in a traffic circle. We are going to bring back all the pieces, each EFP, and crate them up in a wooden box, and put them on the first helo south so they can be analyzed. Unfortunately, despite his best efforts, our robot operator, Mengershausen, couldn't further break up the foam chunks, or rip the wires, or snap the plastic-encased detonating cord. So we are going to have to drive up and then manually cut, disassemble, and grab the pieces ourselves. In the traffic circle. Under the watchful eye of the assembled crowd. Among whom are probably the bombers who put the device there in the first place.

Castleman, Keener, and I made a plan. We're going to drive around to the other side of the cordon, move our security back to protect our rear, and then drive in and pick up the foam remains. As team leader, Castleman will get out with his heavy-bladed knife, cut all the remaining detonating cord currently linking each EFP in a daisy chain, and throw them in a metal ammo can we keep in our Humvee for just such a purpose. I'm going to dismount, stand over him, and cover him with my rifle; if he is looking down at the bomb, he can't be looking up for possible threats. Keener will stay behind the wheel, on the radio, and either call for help or drive us out if things go bad.

It was not an in-depth plan. It may not have even been a good plan. But we had few other choices, with the EFPs a hundred yards away and us at the edge of the security. And it was better than Castleman taking the Long Walk alone, exposed in the open in an eighty-pound bomb suit. This way, at least I could cover him.

We drove across sidewalks and past storefronts, and arrived at our starting point on the edge of the traffic circle. The crowd had not grown bored and thinned; they kept watching, pointing and curious. Our security was impatient, and didn't like being stuck in one spot this long. Neither did we; the longer you stayed in one place, the more time Haji had to find his friends and drop mortars on your head.

Castleman pulled out his knife. I turned up the intensity of the red dot in my electronic rifle sight, so I would be sure to see it in the brilliant sunshine. Castleman's easy smile, his generous Midwestern grin, was replaced with a mask of will.

Keener's constant grimace deepened; little made him happy, this plan least of all. One last breath, Castleman gave the go-ahead, and we drove in.

The Humvee mounted the curb and sped toward our prize. Keener looked for other bombs, hidden away, meant to protect the EFPs or kill us if we got too close. Castleman thought of nothing but cutting apart the remains of the IED as quickly as he could. I scanned rooftops, for gunmen or lookouts. If a sniper was waiting in a dark upper window of a nearby apartment building, I would never see him, even after Castleman was shot and dead. But I could spot other, more conspicuous, threats among the assembled crowd.

Keener screeched the armored truck to a halt, two feet from the foam lumps. Castleman leaped from the front seat, ran to the heavy awaiting chunks, and furiously began cutting. I dismounted, stood over him, raised my rifle, and dared the crowd to shoot. Ninety seconds. That should be all the time we needed.

Most of the pedestrian onlookers at the base of the closest apartment building didn't even move when I pointed my rifle at them. Then slowly, as a trickle, several families turned and left, wishing to avoid the gunfight they now saw coming. Eighty seconds.

I surveyed the crowd again. We were totally exposed at the bottom of the concrete canyon.

Sixty seconds.

I looked up again, scanned the peaks of the tenement complexes, and saw a commotion on the rooftop directly in front of me. Several men appeared and left.

Fifty seconds.

A new man now appeared in sunglasses, stared at me briefly, then turned and left again. They were little more than silhouettes against the harsh bright summer sky. I lost track of all movement on the street, and concentrated on this one building, in view of the EFPs, in view of the traffic circle, the tallest apartment building for several blocks. I waited.

Forty seconds.

"How are you doing down there?" I asked. Castleman was cutting off foam to expose the inner core before tossing each EFP into the metal can. He was up to four.

Thirty seconds.

Three more shapes appeared on the rooftop. Children, young boys, barely older than my oldest son. They had a cell phone. They were pointing and talking. Pointing at me.

Twenty seconds.

I raised my rifle, flipped the lever off Safe, and put the red dot on the chest of the boy with the cell phone.

Fifteen seconds.

Six EFPs in the ammo can and counting. I looked at the boy. He looked at me. I put my finger on the trigger.

Ten seconds.

Ten seconds to get the last EFP. Ten seconds to not shoot this boy.

I counted to eleven, and exhaled.

II | *The Soft Sand*

I GOT MY first tattoo with Jeff Chaney the day before my second son was born. That tattoo eased my son into this world, his mother so angry that she went into labor.

My first tattoo is one day older than my son because Jeff Chaney had convinced me I needed some ink, and that we were going to go together. Jeff's quest for fun had few boundaries and only occasional limits, either personal or actual. He would try anything himself twice . . . and then do anything with you a third time. Jeff's devotion to the savoring of life was infectious and magnetic. He was generous with his time, his friendship, and his alcohol. He did outrageous things with lots of people. I'm lucky that I was around to be a part of it.

Jeff picked out the tattoo parlor on Route 98, the beachside strip in Destin, Florida. Jeff was in the Navy, and several years older than I, had half a career already under his belt, driving boats and ships all over the world. This was not his first tattoo, and he knew what to look for in a good artist.

We spent weeks planning our designs, in between study sessions and ordnance tests. I wanted an upside-down sword with two gas masks hanging from the hilt, one the U.S. Air Force MCU-2/P, the other the round-eyed British mask often caricatured in apocalyptic comic books. I had acquired a couple of masks from my first Air Force assignment, and Jeff and I took countless pictures of them hanging from broom handles on his back porch, ensuring that we got the angles just right to give the tattoo artist the perfect perspective to copy. They reminded me of my time before Explosive Ordnance Disposal school, before my new life. This was my rite of passage on leaving my old world, but I was not yet fully in my new one. I was closing a door behind, but the one in front had not yet been opened to let me in.

Jeff got a huge squid on his calf, and he wasn't worried that the door was still closed in front of him as well. Inside of the sea creature's tentacles he left space for the EOD badge, the Crab, to be placed after he graduated from the school. Actually graduating wasn't a concern for Jeff. Of course he wouldn't actually get the Crab portion tattooed right away. That would jinx it; superstition is ubiquitous among those who work with explosives regularly. Nor would he disrespect the EOD operators that went before him by getting a tattoo of the Crab before he had earned it. But earning it was a matter of when, not if. Jeff had never failed at anything in his life that he put his carefree mind to, and his easy positivity was a delight that drew others to him. Jeff always got the girl, got the boat, got the job, and he would get his Crab. And we did.

I was a snot-nosed, baby-faced, butter-bar lieutenant deployed to Prince Sultan Air Base in Saudi Arabia on a quick ninety-day rotation when the planes flew into the World Trade Center. We watched on TV like everyone else. But once the second tower fell, we turned the TV off and got down to work that I never actually expected to do.

The Air Force was confused about what it wanted me to be when I grew up. I applied for an ROTC scholarship out of high school because I wanted to be an astronaut. None of my teachers had ever broken the news to me that I couldn't fly into space, so the third-grade dream remained. The day the Air Force recruiter came to my high school, I marched up to his table and declared my intent. He looked me straight in the eye, through my thick glasses, lied to me, and said I was a shoo-in. So I took the scholarship to be an electrical engineer, and only when it was too late did I learn that my poor eyesight would ensure that flying in space was not in my future.

But the Air Force didn't want me to be a circuit geek after all. Once I finished college and earned my engineering degree and received my commission, they assigned me to be a civil engineer, pouring runways and fixing buildings. But I never learned how to do that either because upon arriving at my first assignment, I was placed in disaster preparedness, the stepchild of Air Force civil engineering. I taught people how to wear their gas mask and survive nuclear war.

So when I arrived in Saudi Arabia in August of 2001, as there was no chemical, biological, or nuclear war going on, all I prepared for was to be bored until it was time to go home. Obviously, that plan failed. We opened up crates of chemical-agent detectors that had been gathering dust for a decade. We stockpiled bleach to clean up an Al Qaeda nerve-agent attack on Osama bin Laden's homeland. We fired up the biological-agent detectors and ran them twenty-four hours a day. We sat up all night, and watched, and waited, and scared ourselves to death, because there was nothing else to do. I was overwhelmed.

But we weren't the only ones who were worried. One day, several months after 9/11, I was invited to a meeting whose agenda was kept secret. As a young lieutenant, I was not normally invited to meetings like this. I sat in a packed makeshift classroom with several of my fellow chemical-warfare specialists, most of the fire department, a couple of security police officers, and some emergency staff from the hospital. At the front of the classroom, looking out over the group with grim faces and closed mouths, were two guys not in military uniforms. They had hiking boots, tan cargo pants, loose short-sleeved shirts, and beards. At that time, beards were universally recognized code for "I have a job that's special." Sitting in the front corner were several other Air Force guys whom I recognized but did not really know. They stayed by themselves and carried guns, which the rest of us never did. And they had lots of guns, and gear, and over-vests to put the gear in. They talked quietly to the two men in beards before sitting down when the briefing started.

"The reason you are all here," the bearded guys said to the whole group, "is because the United States has intelligence that Osama bin Laden has acquired two of the missing Soviet suitcase nukes and intends to use them. If such a device is discovered, employed and counting down on a timer, there will not be time to call for help. You are all first responders, and so most likely to discover the device. If you find it, you will have to turn it off yourself."

The bearded guys were there to teach us how to do that.

They pulled out a package, as big as a shopping bag and covered in a blanket. Inside the wrapping was a dull green metal cylinder, fat and smooth, except for one flat end that had several dials and switches on it.

"This is a model of the old Soviet suitcase nuke," they said. "And here is how you turn it off."

I sat in silent rapture, and memorized every word. No one in the hall spoke, except for the small group of Air Force guys in front with the gear and the guns. They asked lots of questions, and it sounded like they already knew what they were talking about. This device wasn't new to them. The concept was almost . . . commonplace.

"Those are the EOD guys, right?" I whispered to a fellow gas-mask instructor sitting next to me, looking lost in the details of the complicated shutdown sequencing.

"That's right," was the reply.

EOD. Explosive Ordnance Disposal. The bomb squad.

"And they get to do this all the time?" I asked, mostly to myself.

Now I knew what I wanted to be when I grew up, and I would make the Air Force let me do it.

It took me a full year of begging my commander, pleading with headquarters, and badgering the bureaucratic system to get into EOD school at Eglin Air Force Base in Fort Walton Beach, Florida. But I eventually got my wish, and one chilly January morning, after moving my uneasy wife and growing family down to the Gulf of Mexico, I sat in a plain white classroom with twenty-nine other hopefuls for my first day of training. Only three of us would graduate together nine months later.

In the first three days of class students take three tests. A passing score on every test in EOD school is 85 percent. Many questions are worth sixteen points. You have exactly one day to learn new material that you have never before encountered in your daily life—like how the inner gears and lockballs of a setback-armed, mechanically timed and graze-impact-fired mortar fuze work—and then the next morning take and pass a test. If you fail that test, you may get a second chance. If you fail your second chance, you start that section over again with the next class below you in line. But after that, your third strike, you're out.

EOD school is an assembly line. If you fail your quality check, you may go back through the stamping machine. Fail again, and you get tossed out with the other broken widgets.

EOD school focuses the mind in a way high school or college never did. I never worked so hard or wanted something so much. It dominates your time, your thoughts, your conversations, and every aspect of your life. You arrive before dawn to study, and leave late in the evening long after dinner. The only true day off was Saturday, since Sundays were "optional" study halls; in truth, anything but. The only way to absorb so much material was to think of nothing else. The only way to graduate was to want nothing else.

By the time I was done, the only thing I could imagine doing for the rest of my life, however long that might be, was taking apart bombs.

In my initial class of thirty on the first day of EOD school I was the only commissioned officer. I got used to that pretty quickly, and was often the only officer everywhere I went for the rest of my time in the military. The Navy runs EOD school, on an Air Force base, with instructors of all four services, and students of each branch get mixed together. We had seven Army soldiers, five Navy guys, fifteen other Air Force kids (all but one straight out of boot camp), and two Marines. Four didn't last the first week. Barely half lasted the first two months.

Boatswain's Mate First Class Jeff Chaney was the highest ranking enlisted guy in the class. That meant he was my number two, my partner, my problem solver and my confidant. He also was chief party planner, beer procurer, morale enforcer, and physical-training guru. He led the runs in the morning, and got the kegs for the weekend at the beach. He made sure everyone was studying, that the new kids were staying out of trouble, that the "deck" got "swabbed." He quickly became my best friend.

EOD school builds in complexity and momentum every day. We started with physics and the fundamentals of ordnance: bombs, rockets, missiles, grenades, land mines, and more. Then basic demolitions. Remote tools. Biological and chemical agents. Ground ordnance. Air ordnance. IEDs—improvised explosive devices. And finally, the culmination, nuclear weapons.

Explosive theory becomes practical application becomes physical trial to master. First, the science: how materials detonate. The fine details of the explosive train, starting with a small speck of sensitive compound and culminating in a powerful burst of heat and light, transforming potential into chaos. How detonations are simply supersonic chemical chain reactions. How the speed of the wave flowing through a block of C4 relates directly to the velocity of the frag then thrown by that blast—the chunks of steel, ball bearings, nuts, bolts, nails, or pieces of dead dog now moving at a rate we referred to as Mach Oh My God.

Next, how to harness that explosive power for your own ends. To propel steel slugs, wedges, forks, buckshot, and water into the delicate mechanisms that make ordnance work. To shear a firing pin before it strikes. To unscrew a fuze on a bomblet dispenser. To melt a pressure pad on a land mine.

And most important, to shoot jets of water into improvised devices to tear them apart before they function. When water is concentrated, focused, and directed by explosives, it creates an unyielding blade that rips and pushes without sympathetically detonating an IED's hidden payload. Water does not compress. The wooden boxes, PVC pipes, burlap bags, and sheet metal containers of the renegade bomber all succumb to that universal solvent.

Finally, book learning done, go out to a range and do it for yourself under the unblinking eye of your ever-watchful instructor.

Using what you learned on day 1 to solve a problem on day 4 is hard enough, considering the three tests you have sweated over in between. Applying what you learned in demolitions in month 1 to dissect a Soviet guided missile five months later is more vexing. Students become overwhelmed with the mountain of material, the broad scope, the relentless pace, and the stress. Always more stress. Make a mistake, fail a test. Fail two tests, start over. Fail three, and the dream is done. All your energy, your desires, your focus, revolved around passing the next test.

Everyone had rituals. I had a lucky set of red boxers, ratty with holes, and a lucky pencil, still squirreled away in the back of a dresser drawer in my bedroom upstairs in case of emergency. Some guys always had sex before a test, and some poor saps never did. One guy managed to convince his girlfriend he needed a lucky blow job every time. I started with my wife on the lucky sex, but soon had to give it up with the birth of our second son, post-tattoo. Even so, every night before a test I sat on our bed, closed my eyes, and visualized every step of the next day. Being called by an instructor, walking to the practical area, doing a long-range recon of the Chinese spin-stabilized rocket, choosing a technique to disarm the firing system, placing the explosives. Every step. Blasting cap on time fuze, crimpers on, turn your head, squeeze. Every step. To pass and survive to the next day. For nine months.

You are a different person on graduation day from the day you started. The crucible eliminates self-doubt and instills supreme confidence. The combination of intellectual and physical requirements, academic rigor, emotional stress, and final consequences is unparalleled. It's like being a surgeon, except if you screw up, you die, not the patient.

I entered EOD school a skinny dumb kid who hoped he could hack it. I left a focused, dedicated, obsessive, invincible man whose only purpose was to go to Iraq and blow things up for real.

I'm running again, always running, along the river, down the road from my home, left eye twitching, footfalls on pavement burning away the Crazy in my chest and mind.

I run alone. Ricky doesn't run with me, not yet. Back at Nellis, at my last Stateside assignment, Ricky and Grish and Luke and I and the whole unit ran together almost every day, four miles through the desert on the base's outskirts, staring down the flight line at the Las Vegas Strip shimmering in the early morning sun. Now my feet fall on empty pavement, shuffling stampede an echo, my breath alone in my ears, the road bare ahead and behind.

I push against the mountain of Crazy in my chest and pick up my pace.

Clouds move in, and a sprinkle starts, a drop or two that grows heavier with every step. A block later, steady rain falling, puddles growing along the side of the road. Two blocks later, sheets and standing water in my shoes, plastering my shirt to my back and chest. I grunt. The Crazy bubbles.

————

Tropical Storm Bill was bearing down on Florida, dark and full, as I carried my tools into the practice yard at EOD school. My final test on bombs; the most involved yet. The fuze I had to remove from the back of a two-thousand-pound bomb was long and heavy. Unscrewing one can cause it to detonate, so you definitely don't want to do the work by hand and be around for that. Instead, I would need to construct a complicated series of leads and pulleys with a wrench that operated remotely by pulling a rope. I carried the rebar stakes for the pulley system under one arm, and a sledgehammer under the other, as the rain started to fall.

"We're gunna get this fuckin' test done real quick, you understand? Fuckin' hooyah?" asked my Navy instructor, whom we called Chief Bongo, his actual Pacific Islander name being completely unpronounceable.

Bill grew darker, swirling overhead, and the rain grew in size and intensity.

"Hooyah, Chief," I replied, soaked to the shorts before I had even made it to the bomb.

The fuze had to slide out backward completely straight; cant it slightly at the start and it would jam and get hung up inside. So after attaching the rope-actuated, spring-released mechanical wrench, you have to lay out a series of bungee cords to provide the pulling force to extract the fuze. Then pulleys attached to the stakes guide the rope several hundred feet away to a safe area from which you actually pull. Once the entire system is in place—bungees, pulleys, stakes, and rope—you tug on the line, which after running and switching through several pulleys activates the wrench, which turns the fuze. Once you fully unscrew the fuze and overcome the last thread, the bungee cords yank the fuze out and the test is over.

I struggled at building this Rube Goldberg machine during

practice days. Now, in the middle of my test, Bill was getting angry.

By the time I was done attaching the impact wrench, the bomb was nearly underwater. I picked up my sledgehammer to drive in the first stake and thunder cracked, not overhead, but to our right.

"How you fuckin' doin', Lieutenant! Let's go! Hooyah?" roared Chief Bongo.

"Hooyah, Chief." I swung the sledge and pounded in the first unintentional lightning rod.

The rain came sideways and in waves. Bill darkened the sky as an early night, and lightning jumped from cloud to cloud, striking and splitting pine trees with ear-rattling cracks in the surrounding forest. I pounded in stake after stake and attached pulley and line, water in my eyes, sledgehammer slick, boots soaked, shirt and pants heavy and waterlogged.

Bill was at full roar as I ran the rope through the last pulley and humped the remainder out to my distant safe area. No time to rest, I simply grabbed the rope and pulled. *Tink* went the wrench, barely audible over the fury of the wind in the trees. Heave went the rope. *Tink* went the impact wrench. Heave and *tink*. Heave and *tink*. Heave and silence.

I couldn't see the bomb, low in the water, through the windblown sheets of rain. I was out of breath, my back and shoulders aching from the strain of pulling the rope after driving so many stakes. Nothing to do but pull. Heave, and the fuze stayed stuck. Heave again. The rain ran in my nose and mouth as I put my head down and panted, hands on my knees.

"Lieutenant, finish right fuckin' now! Got it? Fuckin' hooyah!"

Lightning lit up the Chief screaming in the distance, rain lashing his silhouette. I heard him fine, no matter Bill's howl.

I wrapped the rope around my waist, and leaned into the pull. Heave, and wind and water and thunder, but no fuze. It stayed jammed in the back of the bomb.

"Right fuckin' now, Lieutenant! You hear me? Hooyah? Right fuckin' now!"

"Hooyah, Chief." One more heave, one more lean, one more strain. *Tink.* The fuze slid out.

EOD school doesn't just teach the technical aspects of bomb disposal. More important, it instills the culture of the profession.

There is no choice but to work hard. But hard work is not enough. You won't survive EOD school if you can't work with a team, and can't relax when the job is done.

Fortunately, my class naturally banded together, and the beaches and bars of northwest Florida provided ample opportunity to blow off steam. "Cooperate to graduate" is a common mantra, as students test each other and work together to cross each hurdle. Every Friday night of EOD school was a blur of bars, clubs, beer, and few clothes. Many EOD guys prefer to drink with their pants off. Or as a hat on their head. I can't explain why.

It is impossible to overemphasize how important beer is to the EOD profession. Beer at the end of a long week of school, to ease the stress of tests and retests. Beer to quench your thirst from a full day of clearing the bombing range in the relentless desert sun. Beer to dull the pain of a lost brother on the battlefield, near or far, known or unknown. Beer to bond, and celebrate, and mourn, and remember, and forget.

As weekend planner and surrogate older brother for every member of our class, Jeff organized elaborate marathons of fun. Every night ended with holes in your memory, requiring careful reconstruction with the class the next day. Only a few nights ended in a fight with the locals, or being tossed from a bar, wrecking it on the way out. Most nights ended with breakfast, a tasteless plate of grits and waffles, and a ripe hangover to endure on your one day off. Jeff was tireless, relentlessly upbeat, and more than once dragged my exhausted body onto his boat the next day to swim my headache away with the dolphins in the full sun of the Gulf. A quick nap on his couch, and I was ready to party again, this time dancing at the club late into the night.

Jeff was as lucky with women as he was with the rest of his life. Not only did I have to endure fantastic tales of his past exploits, we all had to watch him and his wife together, dancing and partying, at the bar, at the club, on the stage reserved for the most attractive women and guarded by granite blocks of men. Jeff's wife was a vision: sultry, playful, sweet as cantaloupe on a summer day, and hotter than a firecracker. Jeff's lack of inhibitions included public dancing, and his wife had the ability to draw the attention of the entire club to her swaying and dipping form, especially when she was invited onstage.

"Are you looking at my wife?" Jeff would yell at the club, to no one in particular.

Jeff's grin was ear to ear, and his wife gave a devilish smile from above.

"You better not be looking at her," Jeff continued. "She's coming home with me tonight!"

I learned many things from Jeff during EOD school. I learned the best way to bury a keg in beach sand to keep it cool all day long, despite the hot sun. I learned to put skin moisturizer on a new tattoo, but not a kind with aloe, because it might react with the ink. I learned that after twelve hours of drinking, it's possible to fall asleep sitting up, on the toilet, still eating a fast-food hamburger. I learned how to discipline a young enlisted kid without breaking his spirit or breeding resentment. I learned that a certain inlet off Okaloosa Island is a great place to park your boat and watch drunk topless girls frolic in the warm, waist-deep water. I learned to study hard after partying hard. I learned to never give up.

Jeff would lead our class's physical-training sessions a couple of mornings a week before instruction started. I endorsed and needed the workouts; to keep my brain lubricated and spinning, I drank gallons of coffee and ate high-sugar foods all day long. The calories kept my exhausted brain functioning, but they also added to my midsection. Jeff's workouts of flutter-kicks, push-ups, and pull-ups kept the worst of my diet at bay.

The Navy guys had to attend dive school before EOD training, to ensure they could endure the rigors of working underwater. It's difficult to render safe an underwater mine or torpedo if you can't swim in a mask, fins, and rebreather. But dive school is less about learning to use new equipment and more about getting an old-fashioned ass-kicking. The Navy is not going to send you to EOD school unless they are sure you have the endurance, the will, the gumption to handle a certain amount of physical punishment. When I played soccer in high school, if the coach was mad at our performance we would run for hours and never see a ball. In dive school, you swim until you can't move and drift to the bottom of the training pool.

So despite a bit of flab from years of drinking, Jeff could run most of his fellow non-Navy students into the ground. His job leading PT was to bring the rest of us up to speed.

Jeff's favorite morning workout, after an excruciating set

of crunches and flutter kicks, was running the Hill of Woe. Outside of the eastern gate at Eglin Air Force Base are a set of power lines that run up a hill, into the forest, and back through a neighborhood adjoining the base. The three-mile loop up that incline would have been bad, but not epic; no simple slope deserves the name Hill of Woe. But this was Florida— the run was torture because the hill was made of sand. A mile and a half of soft sand uphill.

Up we went, in a line, in step and on pace, singing songs to take the mind off burning calves and thighs. We had done one loop already, but when half of us turned for home like horses that had spotted the barn, Jeff dug us back in and we turned up the hill again for a second round. A third loop for good measure was on its way, but fortunately I did not know that yet.

Up the Hill of Woe, single file in the soft sand. Every step forward brought a half step back as the sand gave way under the weight of our shoes. Ahead of me Shipstead stumbled, put a hand on the ground to steady himself, and then was back up slipping through the viscous silt. My knees aching, my legs on fire, I looked over at the grass on the edge of our running path. We ran up the soft sand path, but paralleling us the whole way, out of the main traffic area, the ground was firmer from plant roots and bits of dirt stabilizing the slope. Would anyone notice? If I ran to the side, just a bit?

I stepped off the soft path and my feet found solid purchase. My backache eased, I stood straighter, and I tore up the hill.

"Whatcha doin' there, LT?" yelled out Chaney.

"I'm coming, Boats," was my sheepish reply.

"Come on, LT. Don't be scared of the soft sand," Jeff called. He was friendly, but firm.

Don't be scared of the soft sand.

My next footfall was back on the path, but it slipped immediately half a foot down the hill. My hips felt the change with a twinge, and my thighs burned anew.

Don't be scared of the soft sand.

Up and down, forward and back, I labored up the hill, in the soft sand, on this lap, and the next.

By the end of school, you have learned the ways of the Brotherhood. When you get the Crab placed on your chest, you have thousands of new brothers and a few sisters. They are unknown but loved. You will travel all over the world together, work together, drink together, laugh and cry and bleed and fight together. You have a new family. They are all that will sustain you.

Jeff died outside of Tikrit the summer after I got back from Kirkuk.

His team got a call that a security unit found an IED on one of the main routes into the city. The security had backed off and set up a cordon a safe distance away. As soon as his armored convoy appeared, as soon as he arrived on scene, there was a massive detonation under his vehicle. It was triggered by a wire concealed in the ground, so his electronic radio jammer couldn't stop it. The unit he was coming to assist never saw the wire or the explosives. Jeff was driving the newest blast-resistant vehicle, with an underbody hull specifically designed to deflect large explosions. But this bomb was almost two thousand pounds of explosives and buried in the road. Nothing can withstand that. His twenty-six-ton assault truck was decimated. The bomber had waited until the EOD team arrived on the scene, had waited while the other security unit unknowingly sat on top of their own deaths, and only triggered his device once the EOD truck pulled up to the exact spot. Jeff never had a chance. I don't know how much there was left to bury.

I have a new job now. Out of the Air Force, out of the military, I'm two weeks into my new civilian life and at my new job, sitting in a bland conference room in a faceless hotel in a blur of a town. I don't know it yet, but there will be a string of identical hotel rooms, a squadron of stuffy airlines, and piles of free continental breakfasts in my future, traveling the country providing last-minute training to EOD guys before they deploy. A parade of faces, a two-week helping of explosives and robots and running drills until they have their tactics just right. Then up and gone, love 'em and leave 'em, to the next half-month stand, another unit, another bundle of hopes and fears. Faces meld and join, till the memory of each brother and sister is just a smear, a lingering haze, a nagging impression. All the faces return. Most alive. Some dead. The list of EOD technicians killed in battle is now largely a list of my former students.

But this is my first job, and sitting in that conference room, fresh and green and ready to teach my first course, that future is still an unknown. I meet my fellow instructors for the first time: John, JB, Jimbo, Vic. Chris and Matt will join the team soon. All former EOD guys, from all four services, done with the military but not done with the Brotherhood; we can't bear that thought so we perpetuate. Everyone has a common acquaintance. War stories start, jokes and outrageous deeds. I know Jimbo from my last tour in Iraq; it is not coincidence, it is a law of averages. So few brothers, there are few degrees ᴄ separation.

And then the news arrives at the conference room. Before I lose a single student, I lose a former classmate. Jeff has died, and so has his teammate Pat. In a truck, on a stretch of deserted highway south of Tikrit. Command wire. Two thousand pounds. Buried in the road.

The Crazy stirs in its sleep. I check my rifle. The foot sits in a box.

I know Jeff. Jimbo knows Jeff and Pat. JB and Vic know Pat. So now I know Pat too, and JB and Vic know Jeff, as the beer flows, and Vic and Jimbo and JB and I remember long into the night.

My wife said she could never imagine Jeff growing old. Now she won't have to.

III | *Failure*

WHAT DO YOU do when your rights are being read? Your legal rights, out loud, to you directly and right in your face, not on television on some crime drama. Do you remain silent? Do you ask for an attorney? Do you yell and scream? Shrink? Run?

I did none of those things. My words failed and my shoulders slumped. The shock made my heart race and my mind spin and my hands shake all the way up to my elbows. I was expecting an ass-chewing, an uncomfortable correction, a warning to never make that mistake again. I was not expecting to be charged with a crime.

When I arrived at my boss's office, a marble-and-plywood box in a captured Iraqi Air Force administration building, I was told to close the door. The First Sergeant and the Chief—witnesses—were standing next to the Colonel's desk, behind and to the side, eyes looking down. That didn't happen during typical ass-chewings. I was asked to hand over my sidearm. I removed my 9-millimeter pistol from the holster strapped to my right leg, released the magazine, popped the round from the chamber, and put it on my Colonel's desk in front of him. That did not typically happen either. The Colonel then looked down, lifted a sheet of paper, and reading word for word in a steady voice, informed me I had been relieved of my command, I had the right to remain silent and any statement I uttered from then on could be used against me in my court-martial proceeding.

The astonishment hit first, but the stoop in my frame did not last. Pride found my spine, confidence my shoulders. As he continued to read, I stood back up, square, at attention, and listened as I was charged with disobeying the direct order of a general during wartime. A crime, if my adrenaline-addled brain could recall correctly, that could send me to Leavenworth.

When he was finished, I ignored my first right.

"Sir, I am very confused. What's going on here?"

The Colonel looked at me with sad eyes. He sighed.

"You need to call the defense lawyer in Germany," he responded.

When I arrived at Cannon Air Force Base immediately following EOD school, I thought of nothing but deploying. Afghanistan was winding down, and the EOD guys there were bored, looking for work. But Iraq was still exciting—the initial push into Baghdad had gone well, and there was a palpable sense that we needed to deploy soon, before all the fun was gone. I saw pictures e-mailed back from guys at the Baghdad Airport of guided missiles, submunitions from the First Gulf War, and piles of artillery rounds being destroyed daily. All the things I had only seen in school were there, spread around the country like trash in a giant landfill. I needed to go before it was all destroyed. It had only taken a year for the good times to end in Afghanistan, and we were afraid we'd miss it twice.

I had only been in my job commanding a unit of about

twenty EOD technicians on the flat, windswept prairie of eastern New Mexico a week before I started calling headquarters, asking when I could deploy next. The gray-haired Chief who endured my begging took my enthusiasm in stride; in less than a year, I was in the training pipeline, the conveyor belt, the cattle chute that leads to the C-130 ride into the box.

I was only beginning to learn about EOD and leadership when my number came, and I had a lot of catching up to do. For all of my self-assured ego and confidence, EOD school really only put tools in my metaphorical toolbox, but hadn't taught me how to use them. Plus, the specific ordnance and devices I encountered in school were quickly becoming obsolete in the war that was developing. The roadside bomb did not fully exist as a weapon in the imagination of the Iraqi insurgent when I completed the IED section of Explosive Ordnance Disposal school. As a student I studied pipe bombs, the Unabomber, and 1980s Eastern European terrorist designs. We investigated the fake training devices using X-rays and a heavy metal disrupter designed during World War II. The robots were old and kept out of the way where the students couldn't break them, and we saw none of the other new technology that was available only months later in Iraq itself. I was learning to be in command, I was learning to shoot, I was learning new equipment, and I was learning a new way of war with everyone else.

EOD had an updated mission. Clear roads, cities, buildings, of IEDs for the grunts and convoys. Find and blow the weapons caches squirreled away throughout the country. Collect evidence from blast scenes to track down and kill the bomb makers. Do all of this while fighting your way through a country on the edge of anarchy. Prepare yourself for the worst. If your security is overrun, and every soldier meant to guard you instead lies rent in pieces, a wet mess strewn about their smoking armored Humvees, be prepared to extricate your EOD team by shooting your way home. No matter what, your brothers come home alive.

Three months before my first real combat tour we began serious deployment workups, leaving home to conduct training we couldn't do at our small base. A week of trauma medicine— IVs, intubations, and tourniquets. Driving our Humvees in a convoy at high speed through mock villages and ambushes. Advanced electronics, to analyze circuits soldered together in dirt-floored caves thousands of miles away. Clearing and rendering safe IEDs with the newest equipment—electronic jammers, British water-and-explosive-mix disruption charges, and sleek robots half the size and weight of the clunkers we had at home—most of which we had never seen before. A combat shooting course, put on by civilian contractors, where we moved and fired our weapons in ways that never would have been allowed by the safety-soaked and risk-averse larger Air Force.

The muddy and ramshackle shooting range looked more like the forgotten corner of an old farmer's property than the scene of advanced tactical marksmanship training. Two picnic tables, a temporary shelter, rows of railroad ties that demarked shooting lanes, a pile of dirt on one side of the long gallery to catch our lead. Located at the end of a winding track off our maps, the contractor's firing range was isolated in the low, thick central Texas woods, wet with November rain.

But initial looks could be deceiving. Piled on those picnic tables, in unmarked separate cardboard boxes, were a hundred thousand rounds of 5.56- and 9-millimeter ammunition. Rifles, pistols, magazines, optical sights, scopes, infrared lasers, drop holsters, cross-draw and multi-mag vests, body armor, helmets, slings, armored gloves, and cool-guy sunglasses littered the surrounding grass, fell out of the back of pickup trucks, and stood ready for use. And at one end, against the dirt berm, were rows of heavy steel targets, some with paper coverings depicting Middle-Eastern-looking men, some blank and naked.

My right thumb was raw from loading magazines by lunch on the first day. To the firing line, for warm-up shots with the rifle and then pistol. Back to the picnic tables for remotivation and magazine reloading. At the firing line again, for transition drills between rifle and pistol. More lectures and magazine loading. To the line again. Three shots with the rifle to the chest, switch magazines, then three more. Professionals do the simple things well: accurate and sustained fire, counting rounds so you are never dry, reloads under fire, immediate actions to fix a broken weapon, transitions from rifle to pistol and back, squaring your body to the threat so your vest absorbs the shock of impact if you are shot, moving and communicating and working as a team while under duress. The *plink* of lead on steel was a soothing song of success.

All the while, our contracted instructor, an ex–Marine Recon trigger-puller, barked, cajoled, mocked, ridiculed, and motivated. A command to the line, to prepare to fire. A call to shift fire, as a new threat emerged. A distracting whisper in your ear while you slowly squeezed the trigger. Grunts and yells and shouts to communicate over the din of twelve talking assault rifles.

The worst of all sins: not hitting the target. "Whatever you do, Captain, don't miss!" came the regular admonishment from behind me.

By the third day, simply killing steel was not enough. We

graduated to battle drills—recovering and tending to a fallen comrade, dismounting a vehicle under fire, entering and clearing a building, moving and evading hostile fire through an organized violent retreat. Peels from the left, peels from the right, Australian in-line peels, shoulder taps and foot pressure to move through a room. Timing reloads to ensure a constant hail of bullets on the head of the enemy.

The upgraded shooting regimen was interspersed with words of combat wisdom from our instructor, aphoristic *hadith* pearls from the master, blessings on the student. We sat at his feet, loaded yet more magazines with row upon row of ammunition, and absorbed the enlightenment. Simple concepts that inspired confidence in ourselves and our ability to return alive.

You must be willing to commit more violence than your enemy. A firefight is a test of wills to kill.

You must mentally prepare to be shot. To absorb the impact, to brace your chest against it, and then continue to return fire.

Live behind your weapon. Take cover behind your weapon. If you are shooting at your enemy, he will put his head down and not shoot back. If he is not shooting at you, you cannot get shot.

Your rifle, your pistol, your vest, your head, and your heart are a five-man team on your side. They will save you. Stay alive no matter what. You don't quit until you are dead.

Always be alert, be present, be ready to kill. When the moment comes, your training and muscle memory will save you.

The last day of training, the final exam, the last shooting sequence, was a combination of all previous exercises. We moved down the grassy field on patrol, soggy scrub trees transformed into dusty crumbling walls of an Iraqi village in my mind's eye. Suddenly, our instructor calls contact front! Twelve of us came on line, and a thousand rounds are fired in the first minute, overwhelming violence perpetrated upon our imaginary foe.

I needed to change mags, and yelled, "Reloading!" over the roar to my right and left. My partner next to me called, "Covering," and killed my targets and his during my five-second change-out. In one rote motion I dropped the old mag with my right index finger, reached for the replacement with my left hand, and keeping my eye on the target and never looking down, inserted the new mag and brought the bolt forward and home. "Up," I shouted, and the fire continued.

A command from the instructor. To my right, DJ called for a peel. One by one, the shooter on the right end of the line called, retreated, turned, and began firing again, into the enemy and past the line in front of him. Yard by yard we retreated down the cobbled Iraqi street.

Then, to my left, Brown fell. Hit. Wounded by a phantom bullet, a shoulder tap from our merciless instructor. He had to be recovered and brought to safety.

"Man down!" I called, and stepped back over Brown's prone body.

"Covering," came the immediate reply, as Olguin and DJ filled my spot, and placed their squared bodies between Brown and the ghostly incoming fire.

I flicked my rifle to Safe and moved to grab Brown from behind, around the chest in a massive bear hug. Hot shell casings, discarded from the relentless protective fire above us, fell in a rain, onto exposed necks and wrists, into armor gaps and down under my shirt. I sat Brown up, reached around, locked my hands, squeezed, and lifted. Five hundred pounds of man, armor, helmet, tactical vest, rifle, and ammunition lurched backward in one heave. We fell in a pile, inches from where we started.

Don't be scared of the soft sand.

I yelled to DJ to help, and Olguin shifted fire to cover his targets. DJ and I each grabbed one of Brown's shoulder straps, and after a quick count to three, surged forward. My left arm nearly dislocated as we fell again.

Our Marine instructor loomed over me and barked in my ear, harassed and mocked, screamed obscenities, questioned my love for my wounded brother at my feet. Would I leave him to die on the battlefield? Alone? Olguin called for a reload and our team's collective fire waned. We had spent five minutes and four thousand rounds retreating a hundred meters down this exposed Iraqi street. Brown was wounded. I was exhausted. Ammo was running low.

DJ found his second wind, and with a cry and a massive pull, got Brown's deadweight moving again to our rear. I latched on, dug my boots into the mud, and tugged as my rifle flopped against my chest. Our firing line retreated again, back to our rally point, to safety.

I fell again, next to Brown as he checked his bruised body, roughed up from the drag. I panted in exhaustion, and DJ came up to pat me on the head.

"Don't worry, sir," he said. "We're all coming home together."

It is at this time, away from family, away from distractions, away from anyone except those with which you will deploy, that the envelopment of the mind occurs. EOD school taught me to want nothing but the life of a bomb technician. Cloistered combat drills taught me to think of nothing but staying alive. I was whisked away into this sublime psychological deployment current, a profound fatalistic insight that further binds you to your EOD brothers and sisters. A collective yielding to luck, to fortune, to Providence, a resignation of self to a timeless continuum of soldiers gone before.

I met Jessie Spencer senior year of college, on the dance floor of a crowded bar. She was wearing tight jeans and drinking cheap tequila and her smile brightened my soul. It was a hot courtship, a quick engagement, marriage only a year later. I needed Jessie down deep in my gut. And yet. So intoxicating was the seduction of my new mistress—drunk as I was on a cocktail of two parts adrenaline, three parts *philia*, one part noble purpose—that I didn't realize I had chosen a new lover until years later. The smell of my wife's auburn hair, the longing of her blue-gray eyes, the heartbeat of my infant son pressed against my breast, all faded into forgotten memory. The daily drumbeat of training for war, planning for war, celebrating and dreaming and devising for war, was incomparably lovely. It consumed all thought and creativity. It engrossed my being. I wouldn't leave it for as long as I wore the uniform, home or away.

My world became narrow and small—the thirty-five other EOD technicians I would deploy with, a base in Iraq, IEDs, the enemy. Who and what you are leaving behind fades nearly unnoticed. Your time horizon begins when you step onto Iraqi soil and ends when you leave. There are no considerations beyond the handful of brothers in the room with you and the next nine months. There is no thought to the consequences of your decisions past that abbreviated timeline, no imagining of what might follow you home. Home is a lifetime away. Your immediate present, your whole world, is the war. That is where you are going, like countless others before you over the centuries, a line of young men from American small towns and European peasant farms, from great Roman cities and Japanese pagodas on terraced mountainsides. Don the armor, mount the horse, and join your brothers in battle.

But before you leave, on a ship, on the jet, marching out of your village in a column down muddy medieval tracts like previous faceless hordes, you celebrate life even as death stalks in your shadow. The strip club filled to capacity every evening, a long day of training on the range giving way to an overtime of partying. Previous nonsmokers bought cartons of cigarettes. The beer and liquor flowed generously. Even the most button-downed spent money they didn't have on stripper after stripper until closing time. And why shouldn't they? They were going to war.

"Are you a soldier, shugah?" cooed the mostly naked girl on my lap.

"Close enough," I replied. She had dark hair, and relied on hard work rather than God-given good looks for repeat business. I liked that.

"Are you all together? There sure are a lot of you," she asked again, making small talk in between songs. I had thrown another couple of twenties down, so she knew she would be with me for a while.

"We are. We're all bomb technicians, and we leave for Iraq in a couple days."

"Well, this place sure was boring till you got here," she lied in a whisper, her lips brushing my ear, soft breath inducing shivers up my spine. She ran her fingers down the back of my head and neck, along my shoulders and torso, and placing both hands on my hips, lifted herself into a straddle across me.

She leaned in, and I could feel the warmth of her breasts through my shirt.

"You guys deserve to have some fun before you go," she breathed.

The bird touched down at Balad just after the New Year. I was fired less than a month later.

My first C-130 ride ever was my flight from Qatar into Iraq. The deployment was still an indistinct dream in my mind until the main lights turned off in the back of the cargo plane. Stark reality suddenly emerged in the form of a dim red glow that barely illuminated the thirty of us packed onto the cloth bench seats. We had crossed over into Iraqi airspace. Safety and comfort and three-a-day beers at Al Udeid were left behind. I half expected surface-to-air missiles to continuously shoot at us the rest of the way in.

The EOD compound at Balad, a sprawling air base an hour's drive north of Baghdad, was everything my romanticized brain had hoped for. Hard against the flight line and taxiway were rows of armored trucks and dingy tents, dry-rotting in the desert heat. A trapezoidal bunker squatted in the center of our camp, a shelter during incoming rocket attacks and a vault for a collection of seized small arms and ammunition. Plywood-decked floors in the tents concealed the lairs of constantly chattering mice, squeaking all day and night. The sticky traps littering every nook and cranny were all that stopped a full infestation, though the screams of caught mice, tearing themselves apart to be free of the snare, kept me up much of the night. My sleeping area was just large enough for a single cot, barely secluded as it was by several sheets hung to provide a modicum of privacy; a spanktuary to jerk off in and not much else. My first morning in country I awoke to the vibration of a mortar detonation on the runway half a football field away, a daylight attack from hills to the northwest. It was so close that the thud of the detonation's compressed-air shock wave, rather than the actual sound of the explosion, startled me awake.

The food was bad. The terrain was desolate. The threat was real—Sunni insurgents outside of the gate were really trying to kill us.

Everything about Iraq sucked. I loved it.

The environment met expectations, but being in command did not. My carefully crafted vision of life as a deployed EOD operator met the practical limits of the Air Force bureaucracy almost immediately. For two solid years I had dreamed of bombs and explosives with a childlike simplicity. Now I was finally here, in the box, living in a rat's nest, mortars coming down, ready to do the job. But instead of working, we waited.

We waited for approval to store our explosives. We waited for permission to dispose of munitions near the busiest airfield in Iraq. We waited for the General to personally approve every off-base mission we were tasked by the Army to complete. If an IED was on the side of the road, and we were called to clear it, we couldn't go unless we asked the General first. I spent my first two weeks of combat on the phone and writing request letters to the General's administrative assistant.

It didn't take me long to stop waiting for or paying attention to the answers. We were EOD technicians. We had a job to do, and I knew better.

The end came when two of our robots broke. We had a large shelter filled with robots, of every make and model, some experimental, some left over from wars past. But very few of the robots were functional, or fit adequately on the specially prepared ramps mounted to the back of our armored trucks. The robots manually disassembled IEDs so we didn't have to;

they kept us alive. They were also in constant need of repair, but the hub maintenance shop was in Baghdad. Getting there required off-base transport—we needed to ask permission for that.

A week before a scheduled convoy, I drafted an approval letter and sent it to the General's aide. No reply.

Six days before the scheduled convoy, I called the General's office to follow up on the letter. I was told to resubmit the form.

Five days before the scheduled convoy, I e-mailed the request again. No reply.

Four days before the scheduled convoy, I called the General's office again.

"Please provide justification for not utilizing C-130 air transit to move the robots," said the General's executive officer.

"Those birds only fly once a day, and get canceled half the time," I replied. "If we drive down, we can turn right around after picking up the new robots. My guys will be back the same day. I need the robots and teams back—I can't afford to have them stuck in Baghdad for three days waiting on a flight."

"Please provide written justification for not using C-130 assets," the General's exec said again.

Three days before the scheduled convoy, I resubmitted the form, with the required justification.

Two days before the scheduled convoy, a third robot broke.

One day before the scheduled convoy, I called the General's office, seeking verbal approval.

"We're currently considering your request," the administrative assistant answered.

"The convoy is tomorrow. We need to know!" I was not patient.

"Please check your e-mail for approval," I was reminded.

The day of the scheduled convoy came. No e-mail. No approval. Three broken robots.

"Are we running down to Baghdad or not?" Hallenbeck asked. Hallenbeck was one of my team leaders short a robot; his was sitting in pieces on the imminent convoy.

"They're leaving in twenty minutes," Hallenbeck reminded me.

I checked my e-mail again, and looked at the phone. I didn't want to know what the answer was going to be from the General. We needed the robots.

"Yeah, go get in the convoy. Hurry up so you don't miss it."

The e-mail from the General's office disapproving the mission arrived an hour after the convoy left. Thirty minutes later, I drove to my boss's office to hear my rights read to me. When the convoy returned later that day, bearing three new fresh robots, I was not at the compound to greet them.

On a clear midwinter day, morning frost yielding to a warming desert sun, the line of townsfolk waiting to vote in their first election stretched down the muddy track bisecting the tiny village. Despite threats and attacks they waited for hours, robes and coverings clutched tight against the chill, to shuffle through decaying schools and crumbling halls, emerging triumphant with a single finger inked blue. On that day, the Balad EOD unit ran calls for twenty hours straight: bombs discovered at early-morning ballot openings, investigations of suicide attacks on lines of expectant hopefuls. On that day, the pinnacle operation of the tour, the EOD teams ran to exhaustion. On that day, I sat in an office and read a book, waiting for my punishment.

We had been preparing for the election from the moment

I arrived in Balad. Initially, polling places had been the target of threats and hoaxes to scare the local populace into staying home. When plans for the election still went forward, the real bombs started showing up. Daisy-chained explosives outside of government buildings along the path where voters would wait their turn. Drive-by shootings and sandbags filled with radio-triggered mortar shells tossed from car windows into the queuing crowds. Car bombs left overnight and timed for poll workers the next morning. All of those and more, the Balad EOD team disarmed, safed, investigated, and prevented. Without me.

On Election Day, I did not lead my men into battle.

Instead of fighting my war, I just sat, alone, quarantined from my brothers, awaiting my fate, an impotent, mute, broken failure.

I sit on the couch at home, dark night filling the picture window behind me, Crazy sloshing in my chest. I stare at the bottles in front of me. *Twitch.* The left eye has been bad today. My relief is spread across the tabletop.

I start drinking as early as I can now, as early as I can justify it. Not every day, but more and more. On the days when the left eye is twitching at its worst, it consumes all thoughts beyond the boiling Crazy. And today is the worst yet. Fluttering and jerking, a pounding pulse under the eyebrow and swish of the lower lid. I'm an animal driven mad by relentless distraction, not of buzzing insects but of my own body betraying me. Uncontrollable. Intolerable. Just like the Crazy feeling.

A couple after lunch. Two bottles of beer before dinner. Twitching through my spaghetti.

Two more during dishes. I start to help with the children's

baths, then give up as my eye distracts me from differentiating between the soap and the shampoo. *Twitch*. Another bottle before the hockey game. *Twitch*. To the couch and more beer. *Twitch. Twitch*.

I don't notice that my wife has already gone to bed. I sit now, alone, and open another. The number of empty beer bottles on the coffee table is growing.

Twitch.

Twitch.

Please let it stop.

Twitch.

I quickly finish and stumble slightly as I put the glass down. The spinning room slows my eye and pounding heart both.

Twitch. Crazy. *Twitch*.

The last beer in the carton. How pathetic would I look to my brothers now? How would I explain it? Drinking to keep my eye from vibrating out of my skull. Alone in the dark. And scared.

Twitch.

Stillness. A fall.

And then nothing.

The scene was no more horrific than normal. Most gas stations in Kirkuk consisted of a man on the side of the road with a jug of piss-yellow liquid and a hand pump. This gas station, however, for police and government officials, had actual in-ground storage tanks, poured concrete islands to pull your car up to, and 1950s-era American rotary-dial mechanical pumps. An inviting target for a suicide bomber. Or two.

This time they got past the fences and guards using fake Iraqi Police uniforms and identification cards. Or they were real Iraqi Police, with real uniforms and badges. It was always hard to tell.

One bomber approached the aging pumps, idling cars, and quasi-important politicians and detonated his ball-bearing-laced suicide belt in the thickest portion of the mid-afternoon crowd. Fortunately for the assembled, though, he was also near a concrete light pole and pump that absorbed most of the explosive energy. The first blast caused confusion, hysteria, and a flood of police and nearby citizens drawn to the scene.

That was the moment the second bomber entered, detonating his belt in the middle of the Good Samaritan crowd. He made no mistakes, and was well clear of obstacles that would mitigate his effect.

The bombers probably hoped that the gas station itself would explode as the result of their attack. But Hollywood lies, and even aromatic, poorly maintained Iraqi petrol pumps won't send up a huge fireball from a small belt or two. Instead, the bombers simply sowed panic, pain, and madness.

I only ever saw one Hollywood-style fireball. In Balad, one year before, on one of the few missions I completed on my brief, aborted tour.

Organizationally, the Balad EOD compound was a virtual hub for five spokes, five combat outposts that relied on the main base for logistical support. I only visited them once, to make the rounds—drop off mail and pick up gear, remind the guys to shave and take a shower, and swap them out, giving them a not always welcome break at the main hub for a while. Delivering the mail in Iraq is not an easy task. Five gun trucks, our EOD Humvee, and hours of planning and preparation were required just to leave the gate. Our security briefed the convoy order, actions to take on stops, the route we would follow—through the village of Al Dineria, where it was either bloody or muddy, according to the First Sergeant in charge— and how we would stop and fight if ambushed.

Bloody or muddy. Al Dineria turned out to be the latter. And how. The potholes in the hamlet's semi-paved streets were the size of moon craters, and we nearly lost the front end of our Humvee in a harmless-looking puddle in the center of the road. The combat outposts where we stopped resembled frontier forts built to fight the Indian Wars in the American West. At FOB O'Ryan, Bradley armored fighting vehicles were lined up against the outer wall every twenty yards, 30-millimeter chain guns pointing out at the featureless floodplain, ready to respond to rocket and mortar fire. At FOB Paliwoda, foot-thick concrete slabs were stacked like LEGO bricks, building walls, roofs, and shelters for each tin can that housed beds or operations centers. And then to our last stop, across the Tigris, on a pontoon bridge only inches wider than our armored truck.

We picked up a package at that last stop. It was a present from the spooks. There wasn't enough space at their FOB to detonate it. Could we take it back to Balad and dispose of it there?

"What is it?" I asked.

The bearded, plainclothed man handed me an irregular black package. It was the size and shape of a football, completely wrapped in electrical tape and incredibly heavy. On one end a small strand of green detonating cord stuck out.

"Don't worry about what it is," the spook said.

"Sorry, man. I can't just blow things up if I have no idea what they are."

Silence from the spook.

"At least tell me how big the bang is going to be."

"Just blow it by itself—you can cap in here," he said, pointing to the little strip of det cord.

My curiosity got the better of me, and an hour later my teammate Finch and I were back at Balad setting up a disposal shot on the abandoned infield between the two main runways, our designated demolitions area, as it was the only empty space on an otherwise crowded American complex.

"What the hell do you think this is?" I asked Finch, who had been around a lot longer than me.

"Dude, I have no idea, but we're moving back," replied Finch. He had attached the blasting cap to the indicated cord as I was setting up a radio receiver that would electronically initiate the explosion.

"How far back do we need to go?"

"All the way back," said Finch, as he hopped in the truck, and we drove off.

I pulled out the heavy green radio transmitter once we arrived at our safe area, a protective shelter a sufficient distance from the freshly dug pit that contained the black football.

"Fire in the hole," I said, far more quietly than usual, as I peered around the steel wall and pressed the final button.

Thunder and hellfire and a plume of black smoke ten stories high. The crack of the shock wave engulfed our metal box and rattled my lungs. The control tower on the far side of the airfield shook. Windows broke in the flimsy, Iraqi-made administrative buildings dotting the complex. Back at the EOD compound, the phone rang about a possible attack on the airbase.

That explosion lived up to Hollywood expectations.

My tour at Balad did not last much longer, though it ended

over transportation paperwork, not detonating unidentified explosives recovered from strangers. For minor offenses in the military justice system, the General plays prosecutor, judge, and jury. For reasons unknown to me to this day, my charge was ultimately reduced and my penalty dropped to a reprimand that would be placed in my official record. The real punishment, however, was my removal from the unit. I was fired, disgraced, headed home on a plane less than a week later. The C-130 ride back out of the box—back to three-a-day beers and sun and safety and little Air Force girls in bikinis by the base pool in Qatar—was the longest, least welcome flight I have ever taken. I landed alone, lucky to be simply bereft of my command and not headed to jail. But I found my blessings hard to count.

When I arrived in Qatar, home of Central Air Forces headquarters, the top engineer on staff met me at the plane. He said there was a change of plans. He shredded my paperwork and said I'd serve out the rest of my tour working for him. My work-release package involved a purgatory of shuffling virtual papers in a cheap office trailer, in the rear with the gear, answering phones and going to meetings and "working issues" and "providing the leadership with an accurate sight-picture" for their metaphorical radar screen. Every day I read the incident reports detailing missions that my brothers in Balad had completed. Every day I dreamed of a return up north that I knew was impossible.

I had a taste of it now. The rifles, armored trucks, love, Brotherhood, detonations, IEDs, camaraderie, robots, bearded special-ops guys, and incoming mortar fire were all really there. I knew the life I wanted was possible in that exploding dustbowl.

I had to get back. I needed to get back. But how?

I dutifully served my penance until one day, four months in and nearly done with my staff tour, the phone rang. It was a fellow EOD officer, the commander of the largest EOD unit at that time in the Air Force, at Nellis Air Force Base outside of Las Vegas.

"When you get back to the States you're moving here to take over for me," he said in a tone that allowed no debate.

"Didn't you hear, sir? I got fired. I'm done," I replied.

"Yeah, we heard what happened. Tell your wife you're leaving Cannon and coming to Nellis as soon as you get back. We'll get you deployed again to Iraq by this time next year," he said, and hung up the phone.

It happened all as he said, and now here I was. In Kirkuk. Knee deep in blood, charred cars, yelling Iraqi policemen, and sporadic gunfire. Luckiest son of a bitch I knew.

I checked the date on my watch. I landed back in the box a month ago.

One month. I had survived a full month, in command, without getting fired. And I wouldn't be.

"Hey, guess what?" I called over to Ewbank, who was sifting for explosive evidence through a mix of gasoline and unidentifiable body parts near the base of a white petrol pump.

Ewbank looked up. His face was equal parts red and black.

"I made it thirty days without being fired."

"Very groovy, sir!" came Ewbank's chipper reply. He had left his Elvis sunglasses back at the compound, but the cool attitude was perpetual.

We both laughed, and recognized our good fortune, and continued combing through the burned car parts and piss and brake fluid and odd fingers and ball bearings and shredded clothing, looking for omens in the entrails.

I step out of my home, sun shining, air crisp and cold, Crazy on a slow boil, a pot left on the stove all day bubbling and cooking. Another run, to tame the balloon stew, to burn off the worst of the wave overwhelming my life.

Ricky is waiting for me at the end of the driveway. We don't always run together, but he is joining me more and more. Rare is the day now I run alone, and Ricky is a good companion. We don't have to make regular plans; he doesn't need a specific invitation, and is rarely unwelcome. Running to burn off the Crazy can be lonely, and Ricky loves to run. I meet him at the road, and we turn toward the river, wide and gray on this late November day.

Ricky is a broomstick with knees and elbows. Taller than me and with far longer legs, his natural gait is a steady lope I struggle to keep up with. We settle into a rhythm of breaths and footfalls, faster than I would run naturally. But Ricky knows the harder I work the more Crazy I smother, and he keeps the pace up. Two miles in, despite the level pavement and still-warming sun, I'm struggling to keep up. Ricky turns and looks over his shoulder, eyes squinting against the glare and an easy mocking smile on his lips.

"What's wrong, Captain? Don't be scared of the soft sand," Ricky laughs.

I dig deeper and catch up, and soon we are side by side once again.

The road winds between the water and stately homes, snapping nautical flags on beached boats and trim black-shuttered colonials overlooking the Niagara River. Two miles turns into three. Three into five. The Crazy began to loosen its grip at mile four. The last half is comparative bliss.

Ricky and I turn for home, race in a bit of a sprint at the end. Ricky wins. He always does.

"See ya tomorrow, sir." Ricky waves and jogs away fading down the street. I pant, struggle up my driveway, open the door to my house, and the unwavering Crazy engulfs me anew.

iv | *The Daily Grind*

THE REHEARSED BALLET began when a call came in. A bomb squad doesn't drive around town all day searching for IEDs any more than firefighters patrol the city streets looking for plumes of smoke on the horizon. Instead, the entire compound waited in perpetual anticipation, one ear trained for the phone, muscle and concrete taut in preparation, a coiled spring. Armored trucks lay in wait in the yard, noses toward the gate, robots loaded, explosives stowed, doors open and adorned with body armor and helmets at the ready. Teams sorted gear, packed and repacked, checked and rechecked. Every day the explosives were inventoried and refreshed. Every day the robot batteries were swapped through the trickle charger. Every day the jammer was turned on and cycled, load set confirmed. Every day the bomb suit came out of each truck, to inspect the pants and suspenders and spine guard, the zipper and ties, the diaper that swaddles your groin, the heavy overcoat and front Kevlar plate, quick-release tabs, helmet and air snorkel, microphone and power-fan electrical connections, a line of fresh batteries and a wipe of the two-inch-thick visor.

Everyone had a different ritual. No one started a task they could not quickly put aside. Some cleaned their rifles over and over again. Others fretted over the last e-mail from their wife or girlfriend. Mengershausen slept, with one eye open and a black watch cap on, even in the heat of the summer. Ewbank slipped on wide black sunglasses and a Hugh Hefner silk robe, proper loungewear, he called it, took a seat to wait with a cup of specially prepared fancy coffee and *Magnum, P.I.* reruns. Keener pored over supply inventories and bitched that no one completed their paperwork right. Mitchell and Crisp, black and white partners in crime, smoked and joked the minutes away in front of the HAS. I endlessly read reports, wrote reports, rewrote reports, and justified not having to write reports. It filled the time between phone calls, and beat the slow death waiting brings. The ops desk, continuously manned, existed simply to answer that phone. For a call.

Sometimes there was a warning of a call—thunder in the distance on a clear day, a black cloud hanging over the city. Usually we were not so fortunate. Monotony, a string of tasks, the long wait, and then, piercing the quiet, a ring. The ring. Time to go on a call.

If I close my eyes now and let my mind drift I can see every ritualized movement, every inch of concrete crossed, every step between my desk and the waiting armored truck. The papers thumbtacked to the plywood wall next to the phone, the computer that printed maps of the location of each call, the dust on the gray floor, the placement of my pistol in the gun rack, the metal peg on the HAS blast doors where my body armor hung, the contents of every pocket.

My brain has been torn and ripped by explosions, memories of my children stolen or faded, blown apart in each blast. So how do I remember every inch, every second of the move to a call? I am surrounded by reminders. They come unbidden, springing to mind. Every pair of boots I own are sandy. My rifle is always waiting for me. My children's first steps are my walk to the truck.

When the phone rang, and we knew it was a call, I began the rite. Out of the office that I shared with the phone and the ops desk and the big map of Kirkuk on the wall. A yell to the team on standby: time to wake up, time to go, time to do the job. To the gun rack, where I unbuckled my pants and tucked in my long desert camouflage blouse to get it out of the way. Nine-millimeter pistol first, stuck in the back of my trousers. Rifle next, out of the rack, in my hand, then out of the ramshackle work space and into the wide-open covered aircraft shelter we used as our base. Across the dirty floor, past the racks of spare robots and radios and .50-caliber sniper rifles. To my gear, rifle down, pistol out. Body armor on first, lashed across, shoulder armor strapped in place. Tactical vest on top, covered in pouches and pockets containing six rifle magazines, extra pistol mag, flashlight, crimpers, Leatherman tool, knife, a note from my wife begging me to come home, the rosary from my dead Aunt Mary and a scapular, so when I died I wasn't going to Hell, no matter what I had done on the call. Pistol in the cross-draw holster on my front left side. Helmet on my head. Gloves on, earplugs in, sunglasses. Rifle magazine in, bolt forward, round in the chamber.

I could do it today. I do it every day.

Then back to the ops desk—where was the IED, the car bomb, the crater in the road left from a blast that just hit one of our convoys? Map in hand, we talked. Hey, we were just there yesterday. Do you remember the second pressure-plate-actuated device, hidden where we planned to work? That is where Ewbank got hit. That's our third truck bomb in that neighborhood this week. Grim pins stuck in the wall-sized map of Kirkuk reminded us of each call.

The calls come all day and night. Rockets in the morning at breakfast. Car bombs all afternoon. In between prayer times, sung from the minarets. After dinner as darkness sets in. After curfew, when all average citizens should be home snug in their beds, and only trouble awaits on patrol.

Trey said it's not today until you sleep. Sometimes, when the calls pile up, you can go from yesterday to tomorrow and never get to today.

Dawn and a wakeup, tepid mushy oatmeal, a run to clear a crush switch and a couple of 130s left from the night prior, hardened hamburgers on dry stale buns, the regular afternoon suicide car bomb downtown at a school or police station, the weekly serving of pork adobo, dusk, a suspicious-looking white trash bag called in by a hesitant patrol that turns out to be nothing, midnight chow of rubbery steaks and pancakes, an endless drive out and back at twenty miles per hour to a cell phone and dual-tone multi-frequency decoder-board setup discovered by a long-haul convoy in the dark and distant desert, dawn, breakfast of spicy sausage patties and cold omelets, a cordon-and-knock takedown of a weapons cache in downtown Hawija, more hardened hamburgers, and finally, exhausted and delirious, sleep.

It was never today. It was only yesterday and tomorrow.

The worst calls are the ones just after midnight and in the earliest pre-dawn. Sometimes you just know a call is coming. You can feel it in the air; your Spidey sense tingles. Maybe it was a quiet day. Maybe it was good weather; Haji doesn't like the cold or the rain, so a long hot quiet day means a long hot busy night. When you know a call is coming, you stay up late, waiting for it. No point in going to sleep if you are just going to be woken up. But then a call doesn't come. 2200. 2230.

"Hey, Price. Do you think we're getting any calls tonight?" you ask.

"Nah, why don't you hit the rack," answers Price, a hovering mother hen in a linebacker's body, massive black arms the size of your thighs crossed over his wide chest while reading intel reports. Price guards the phone each night, and suffers worse insomnia than you.

"I'll stay up a little longer and see." So you wander over to the adjacent room, and play a little Halo. Every alien is a bad guy, and needs to die. It's so refreshingly simple. Now it's 2300. 2330. Still no call. But you can't hang on any longer; your eyes are closing on their own.

"Price, I'm bushed. I'm giving up for the night."

"Sounds good, sir."

A half hour later, Price is banging on your door with a call. A string of pressure-switch contacts Christmas-tree-light-style and two 122-millimeter projos on Route Cherry. So you roll off your cot and start the ritual: gear on, grab a sugar-and-caffeine energy drink, hop in the Humvee, slam the sickening concoction in one gulp, a stomach rumble, open the door, puke onto the awaiting dirt, and you're ready to run all night long, on a half hour of sleep.

And out you go, out of your compound, off the FOB, outside the wire, past the guards and spotlights and blast barriers and gates, and into the unknown.

What do you think when you leave the gate? When you leave the protected enclosure and false security of your ringed base? I thought of an uncle, filling a C-130 with bullet holes over tiny jungle airstrips in Laos, Cambodia, and Vietnam. A grandfather who built the double runway on Guam in 1944. Another grandfather who landed in southern France and marched to Berlin. A great-great-grandfather, a lumberjack and pig farmer in North Pine Grove, Pennsylvania, fresh from the boat and the Kaiser's army, who at the age of forty-one, and with seven (of his eventual nine) children at home, left his plow in the field to march south with the 63rd Pennsylvania Volunteers, to the Peninsula Campaign and the Second Battle of Bull Run. He returned ten months later, with a bullet hole and a Purple Heart. How would I return?

Thoughts drift further, as the dust and palm groves and empty desert landscape crawl by outside the thick windows of the armored truck. Does the thin line go back further? How far? What blood runs in my veins? Am I from a Line of Old? What may rise in me, unbidden and unknown, to meet this oldest of challenges? How many battlefields has my blood made wet, in empires made and gone, on bare green islands and cold forested mountains of myth, in lands whose names have changed countless times? How many arrows have I dodged? How many rifles have hung from my shoulder? How many bandages have I wrapped? How many helmets have I worn? In the line of my people, all the way back to the beginning.

What resides hidden within me, lying in wait to be revealed, once the cycle continues and renews?

In the darkness of my bedroom, at night, when I try to fall asleep, the top of my head comes off. My chest fills and floats, the ceiling crushes down, and my head cracks open. In a clear line, from temple to temple, around the back of my skull, it lifts free. I can feel it release and open. The spider crawls off the back of my head and runs to the ceiling. I feel every leg detach, as the body forms from the rear cranial knob, and the massive gray hairy spider runs across space and walls and over the foot sitting in a box in a corner.

Living with the Crazy feeling is intolerable. When I awake in the morning, I open my eyes and try not to move. It is the only time all day that the Crazy feeling is not overwhelming and all powerful. It hasn't had time to build throughout the day, and for a brief second, it lies still. I wish my whole day could be that first split second.

Instead, my first thought is always the same. Will I be Crazy today?

And the answer is always "yes" before my feet hit the floor, children screaming, wife rushing to dress for work, my day an agonizing marathon of eye twitches, rib aches, heart gurgles, and chest fullness until I can struggle back to oblivion again, in that bed, eighteen hours later.

When I make breakfast for the children, I feel Crazy.

When I drive them to school, I feel Crazy.

When I sit in front of the computer, fixing PowerPoint slides, I feel Crazy.

When I wait for dinner to finish cooking, I feel Crazy.

When I get on a plane, I feel Crazy.

When the foot sits in the box, I feel Crazy.

When I read my children a book before bed, I feel Crazy.

When I lie next to my wife at night, I feel Crazy.

And then I fall asleep and do it all over again. Why?

The Crazy feeling distracts from every action, poisons every moment of the day. It demands full attention. It bubbles, and boils, and rattles, and fills my chest with an overwhelming unknown swelling. My misery compounds.

I wake every morning hoping not to be Crazy. Every morning I am. I grind through. Month follows month.

This is my new life. And it's intolerable.

I can't do this.

I hated going out at night. Our security hated going out at night too. Yes, we had all the fancy NVGs, our night-vision goggles, and other gear so we could "rule the night," as the grunts liked to say. But we didn't use them because we had to drive in downtown traffic, and we'd hit every civilian vehicle between us and the IED if we didn't turn on our headlights. So instead, in the worst possible combination of circumstances, the bad guys got to hide in dark houses, and we had to drive with two bright white targets on the front of our Humvee, and two red ones on the back.

A call came in from Cougar 13, a regular infantry patrol, for a bomb on the big bridge spanning the Khasa River, just a tiny stream at that time of year that trickled through the center of Kirkuk from north to south. The big bridge, a glowing target visible from miles around, above the dark gash of rabbit warrens and wadis.

At least it was a respectable hour, not long after full dark. This night the patrols got out earlier and found the IEDs quicker, so my teams and I were still awake. Which meant the city and Haji were still awake. A city of a million Arabs and Kurds and Turks, ancestral homelands for each, depending on which century you consulted. The Kurds were the best organized, controlled the levers of official political, law-enforcement, and military power, and had a plan for restoring Kurdistan: outbreed their neighbors. Arabs who had relocated to Kirkuk during Saddam's rule did not take kindly to bullying eviction, and sympathized with the terrorist networks that retaliated. The city's gory present conspired to spoil the city's hopeful future, so prodigious the blood soaking into the ground that it contaminated the oil reserves hidden beneath the rocky desert.

Four armored Humvees pulled into the parking and staging area in our compound, right in front of the HAS. After donning our helmets, sandy Kevlar hiding Castleman's sandy blond hair, we walked up and met the security lead, Bayonet 23. Bayonet didn't normally take us out. It was usually Psycho, the mortar platoon. But Psycho was on a personal-security-detail mission with the brigade commander, and Bayonet was stuck with us. Or we with them.

We shook hands, bullshitted, and looked at the map to figure out where we were going. It was our job to clear the IED upon arrival, and Bayonet's to get us there and keep us alive while we worked. We had done it many times before, but this time there was one wrinkle—we had a passenger. The Colonel, my boss, was nervous about our overall mission. He couldn't figure out what we did. He didn't understand why Air Force guys were driving around on the ground with the Army, where they could get hurt. He didn't understand that EOD technicians from all four services were nearly interchangeable, received virtually the same training from the first day of school. He didn't understand that the stenciled "U.S. Air Force" name tapes on our uniforms signified little to us. He didn't understand that we were now more comfortable with the Army, had more in common with the grunts who went outside the wire every day than the wrench-turners and computer junkies who stayed on their safe air base. He wanted to come see for himself, and I couldn't tell him no, so he had waited all day to get a call himself. This was his chance. He stood an attentive distance away from our powwow and didn't ask any questions. When we broke and mounted up, I put him in the back right seat, where he was less likely to get killed.

Our convoy of five armored trucks drove off from the compound to the FOB gate, popped on the jammer, locked and loaded our weapons, and thundered out the serpentine, out of the wire, and immediately to the right, joining Kirkuk's unceasing traffic midstream. South down Route Cherry, then left at the auto dealership, where we had investigated a car bomb a couple of days prior. We drove in the middle of the road, as fast as the Humvees would go, local cars pulling to the side to avoid being overrun. Stopping is dangerous and so to be avoided, but to evade collisions, all civilian traffic must pull aside when you need to change course. The front gunner carried a dazzling green laser and would flash it in the eyes of oncoming motorists when we had to make left-hand turns against traffic. Everyone stops driving when they can't see. Thus did our armored convoy barrel toward the western base of the bridge, parting a sea of jammed, congested humanity. The Colonel just sat, his tall frame wedged uncomfortably between his armored window and our robot control station, gripping his too-clean rifle unfamiliarly, staring at the city going by. He had never been off the FOB before.

Cougar 13 and several of their Humvees were already waiting for us in an empty lot at the base of the bridge when we arrived. We eased our armored truck up to the inner command vehicle, parked, and Castleman dismounted to query the sergeant in charge of the cordon.

No, this wasn't their normal sector, they were just returning from a patrol. Yes, they had blocked off all traffic, both this side of the bridge and the other. No, they didn't mark the IED. Yes, it was definitely on the bridge, though it was dark when they found it, and they weren't sure where. What did it look like? A pile of trash. Good, that should help. There wasn't too much trash littering the side of every road in every town of this god-forsaken country. Fuck me.

I got out and peered down the road, out over the bridge that reached into the darkness. Gunfire popped in the distance and occasionally tinged and zipped off the truck or nearby abandoned buildings that were more rubble than intact. The harsh headlights of the Humvees glared in our face, so the remaining deep black night beyond swallowed the bridge whole. I put my hand out, blocked the worst of the direct beams, and drank in the twinkle and shimmer of the city on the other side of the wadi. White and yellow streetlights, with the occasional reddish-white muzzle flash of small-arms fire, followed by a *ping* or two nearby. Flame jumped from a snub-nosed automatic machine gun above me and to my left, as a Cougar turret gunner tracked the flashes from the incoming, and soon it paused again.

Castleman wanted to drop the robot here and send it up into the inky blackness of the bridge to search for the IED with its small cameras and lights. I didn't disagree. It was my team leader's job to run the mission. It was my job to run everything else.

Turning to go back to the Humvee to build an explosive charge for the robot, I bumped into the Colonel instead.

"What's going on?" he asked.

"Please get back in the truck, sir."

"Why?"

"Because we're getting shot at."

The Colonel looked shocked and confused, but complied, turned around and crawled back in. After putting a mandatory cigarette in my mouth, I dug in the back of our truck, found an old plastic Gatorade bottle filled with water and explosives, set it up to detonate, and handed it to the robot.

We employed a variety of robots, each fitting a specific mission need. PackBots were small but maneuverable, light enough to be carried short distances by one man, with a four-jointed arm and multiple camera systems. The Talon was rugged and durable, bigger and heavier but stronger too. Our largest robot was the F6A, nearly four hundred pounds but also practically indestructible, strong enough to lift a hundred-pound tank round, with excellent lights and cameras. Everyone had their favorites. In the dark, with an unknown IED, Castleman picked the F6A.

The stainless-steel robotic gripper latched on tightly to the explosive charge I offered it, our robot driver Mengershausen deftly snatching it via the control station in the Humvee. Each robot was paired with its own flip-open control unit, an LCD television screen, and dashboard of joysticks, dials, toggle switches, and remote-firing systems that allowed a human driver, protected in an armored Humvee, to guide the robot's movements and see what the robot sees using a variety of cameras. It was a disorienting experience, no depth perception at all and spatial awareness at a premium, unless you practiced regularly and honed your skills. Thus each team had one dedicated robot driver, who thought of little else. Quiet, soft-spoken, watch-cap-clad Mengershausen was this team's operator.

I waved into the robot's tall mast camera, indicating he was clear to send the mechanism downrange. The F6A rumbled down the road and over the bridge, searching for our mysterious pile of trash.

Seconds turned into minutes. Minutes piled up. Plenty of trash, but none hiding a bomb. The robot had dug through its eighth pile of innocuous dirt when Castleman started to get frustrated and called Cougar 13 on the radio.

"Where's the fucking IED?" he politely asked.

"You mean you can't find it?"

"No, we can't find it."

"Well. . . ." There was a pause on the radio from Cougar 13.

"Maybe it's closer to the other end of the bridge," Cougar 13 finally replied.

The bridge over the Khasa was half a mile long. Our robot's range was much less than that. We couldn't get to the bomb from where we were. Our security had driven us to the wrong side of the bridge.

The sweltering darkness of the desert night was starting to press in as the sweat dripped down my face, to the end of my nose, and then onto my rifle, hanging down the center of my chest. There was a restlessness to the air, an agitation vibrating through the city. The gunfire was increasing from the other side of the wadi. The honking of horns in the traffic backup created by our security blockade was increasingly agitated. Shouts and gunshots would occasionally startle from behind, or to the side, and then stop suddenly. A crowd had begun to form at the edge of the security cordon, onlookers that talked on cell phones, yelled after their children, barely flinching at the sound of the gunfire. At times, Kirkuk can be a peaceful town, high and dry in the north Iraqi uplands. But at night, the city sometimes transformed, turned, became a thing alive. The tension in the air was rising, a tingle on the scalp. You could feel it grow angry, violent, uncontrolled, edging to a riot. It's exhilarating and terrifying to be the focus of a city's tentacled hate. This whole town was about to go bat-shit crazy, and we were on the wrong side of the bridge.

"What do you want to do now?" I asked Castleman.

"We need to get on the other side of the bridge, and it'll take too long to drive around," he responded.

He was right—the detour to the other side of the river was several miles, and almost an hour's drive in nearly unmoving traffic.

"So you want to drive across the bridge?" Was I actually asking this?

"That's right."

"Past the IED we can't find and through the small-arms fire?"

"Got a better idea?" Castleman's tone was final.

In point of fact, I did not.

Several minutes later we remounted to drive across the bridge, our robot re-stowed and explosives tossed in the back of the Humvee. The rest of the Cougar 13 element was already waiting for us, having spent the last hour holding up traffic on the eastern end of the span. The Colonel, who had been waiting patiently inside the truck with Mengershausen, looked at me and gave an "Are we really driving over that?" look. I nodded. And with a quick extinguishing of our headlights, we plunged into the deep surreal.

We crept forward, the bridge decking rising steadily ahead of us, a slightly lighter gray against the impenetrable night sky. The gunfire on the opposing bank was constant, but no longer directed at us, as we took the long drive alone and unlit. The occasional ricochet pinged off the top of the truck, an annoying buzzing insect just out of reach. Keener looked forward as he drove. Castleman and Mengershausen scanned the front and sides of the road for our suspicious pile of dirt and trash. I stared at the jammer.

All IEDs fall into one of three basic categories: victim-operated, timed, and command. This one probably wasn't set to go off when someone stepped on it or drove past, or else it would have been tripped when Cougar 13 found it. It also probably wasn't time initiated, a tactic normally reserved for attacks on large infrastructure. A device this small wasn't going to bring down the bridge, and how did the bomber know when we'd drive by? That left command, meaning that the bomb was waiting for a signal to detonate. A power dump via a long copper wire. Or a call from a cell phone. Or a code transmitted on a walkie-talkie. Even Iraqi security would have noticed a guy stringing a half mile of lamp cord along the bridge railing, so command wire was probably out. That left radio transmission as the most likely scenario. We had one defense against this threat, and I was monitoring it now.

The green LED display continuously flickered through its cycle as we slowly inched up the bridge, the jammer scanning and monitoring and broadcasting its drowning tone thousands of times a second. The tiny readout, a sick joke by the designing engineers, provided precious little information. Just a string of numbers to be dissected and fretted over.

1 2 3 4 5 6 7 8 9 10 11 12 13 14 1 2 3 4 5 6 7 8 9 10 11 12 13 14 1 2 3 4 5 6 7 8 9 10 11 2 12 13 14 1 2 3 4 5 6

Each number a channel, each channel hit in sequence, each digit a different threat frequency momentarily squashed. The numbers flicked by so quickly I could barely discern them.

7 8 9 10 2 11 12 13 14 1 2 3 4 5 6 2 7 8 9 10 2 11 12 13 2 14 1 2 3 4 5 2 6 7 8 2 9 10 11 2 12 13 2 14 1 2 3 4 5 2

"I think we're getting closer," I called up to Castleman.

6 7 8 9 2 10 11 2 12 13 2 14 1 2 3 4 2 5 6 2 7 8 2 9 2 10 2 11 2 12 2 13 2 14 2 1 2 3 2 4 2 5 2 6 2 7 2 8 2 9 2 10 2

"We're almost on top of it."

Two little metal boxes in our truck, two innocuous antennas mounted on the exterior hardened skin, matching wits with someone hidden trying to kill us as we drove. Could he hear our truck? Could he see us? A glint off our reflective head-lights providing a lethal clue?

Soon we came upon, and nearly hit, some abandoned cars left in the roadway. When Cougar 13 evacuated the area, not everyone took their ramshackle Vauxhalls with them. Slowly we swerved around these cars and trash, threading a needle of potential car bombs, nearing the top of the span, looking for the bomb that must be close, when our driver stopped short.

"Dude, why are you stopping?" I yelled up to Keener.

"There's a guy pointing a gun at me!"

"What?!" Castleman and I dismounted into mayhem. A crowd of Iraqi Police were milling about on the top of the bridge, their American partners nowhere to be found. Light blue police uniform shirts untucked, clutching their dirty AK-47s, the IP looked lost and confused. I don't speak Arabic, and our terp was safely back with the Bayonet 23 security detail at the base of the bridge. Castleman leaned his blond head back into the truck and picked up the radio, scream-ing and incredulous that an IP patrol would be stranded on the bridge next to an IED and inside of a supposedly sealed cordon. The police had obviously independently discovered the bomb and had been guarding it, waiting for us to respond. Now they were lost in the middle of a firefight with no radio communication, stuck on a bridge between two American security teams that would shoot them if they approached. I would have laughed if I wasn't stuck on the bridge with them.

I waved at the IP to follow me as I took cover behind an abandoned car, putting the beat-up sedan between me and the threat: an unfound IED to my front and gunfire on the far right bank. Several IP approached hesitantly, more nervous about me than the chance of getting shot out in the open on the top of the bridge. *Insha'Allah*.

"You need to get off the bridge," I yelled over the drone of our Humvee's diesel engine.

I received blank stares in return. I tried again with a mixture of sign language and basic English.

"Big Boom!" I said, and pointed further ahead. They started arguing among themselves, pointing at either end of the bridge. This wasn't working.

I then noticed one policeman, quieter and standing to one side, who looked out of place. A bandanna on his head, and a face a little too clean shaven. A navy blue shirt, too dark. No moustache, and a paler face. Not Arab. Not Kurdish. Turk? American spook?

I went with my gut.

"You need to get these guys off the fucking bridge right now. That way." I pointed behind me.

"Mista, Mista!" he responded back, shaking his head and putting up his hands in a sign of incomprehension. But the "mista"s didn't sound right either. I looked at him, and he back. A blink. And then he was off, yelling at the IP to follow, down the bridge behind us. The spook vanished.

"What the fuck was that about?" Keener asked.

"They're lost." So are we. "Let's go."

Again we remounted, and resumed slowly crawling forward, peering at the fuzzy grays and blacks of the dark roadway, the green flicker of the jammer lighting up the inside of the truck. Castleman was radioing to Cougar 13 on the other side of the bridge, coordinating and clearing our approach, when Keener suddenly veered to the right, off the center stripe of the road where we had been driving, and buried the gas pedal, tearing toward the brightening headlights of the awaiting soldiers. I guess we found it.

I quickly looked out my window and down. There it was. A pile of garbage just a little different than every other pile of garbage. A wire looped out of the trash. A rounded metal curve in the otherwise random jumble. A pile of refuse like all the others on every street in this city . . . except this one contained enough explosives to kill me where I sat. Inches from my door, from my feet and legs and heart. The other piles of trash in this city could contain an IED. This one actually did. The sure proximity was unnerving no matter how many times I endured it. The bomb lay right *there,* next to me, out my window, waiting.

Keener flipped a U-turn at the end of the bridge and buried us amid the welcoming blanket of the far-side security. I redeployed the robot, grabbed another explosive water bottle, and soon it was working its way toward the pile of trash we had spotted. This side of the bridge was freer of small-arms fire but just as rowdy, a crowd of honking horns and headlights and empty bombed-out apartments looming over us. A dark single-family home with an open mouth lay to our right. I peered into the open door, saw movement, blinked my eyes and shook my head, and it was gone. We needed to clear this IED and be done.

Castleman called out that the robot camera had found our prize. I turned back to the Humvee, and watched through the controller screen as the robotic claw closed on a small two-way radio and started to pull. Motorola 5320? 8530? I'd have to check later, when we wrote the report. Normal setup for the radio bomber who worked in this area was a crude mechanical timer as a safety backup, a nine-volt battery, and a single electric blasting cap. The robot arm lifted and extended, revealing just that: radio connected to battery connected to cap connected to a heavy gray 120-millimeter mortar shell. The Colonel was leaning forward, transfixed, staring at the flat screen, its eerie light iridescent in the deep night. Now to place our explosives, blow everything apart, and get out of here. None too soon.

I went to the back of the truck to prepare our charge for detonation, and instead saw our security trucks, which had been blocking traffic, starting to line up in a convoy formation. To leave. They can't leave—we're not done yet.

"Why is our security leaving?" I called to the front of the truck, yelling to make myself heard over the constant diesel din.

Castleman grabbed the radio and had too short of a conversation.

"Cougar 13 says they've been fragged to investigate a car bombing in the Kurdish market on the north end of the city," Castleman yelled back.

"Why are they leaving without us? We're the ones that do the investigation!"

Castleman laughed.

"Tell them to stop. We're not done here!"

There was another short pause, and then Castleman started swearing and hitting the radio handset against the side of the Humvee in frustration. My turn, to see if an officer talking sense had more effect.

"Cougar 13 . . ." I needed a call sign. What number do Army commanders take? "Cougar 13, this is EOD 6. Where are you going?"

"EOD 6, Cougar 13. FOB Warrior TOC has fragged us to Mike Echo 4473 2681. VBIED detonation, over."

"You are our outer security. You aren't leaving."

"EOD 6, Cougar 13. Bayonet 23 is going to handle your security."

VBIEDs—Vehicle-Borne IEDs, pronounced Vee-Beds—always got the command post excited, thus the urgent change of plans. And Cougar 13's point made sense; Bayonet 23 came with us, after all. Their swap might even have worked under normal circumstances. Tonight, though, there was a bridge, gunfire, and a still-live IED between us and Bayonet 23. If Cougar 13 left, there would be no one holding off the mobs pressing against the security line on this east end of the bridge. We couldn't disarm bombs and be riot police at the same time.

"Cougar 13, EOD 6. Negative. You are staying put until we're done with this one. Then you can take us to the VBIED blast site."

The radio went quiet for a moment. Follow the TOC's direction? Or disobey their ops center to follow my order from the field? Tension filled the line.

"I'll call the FOB Warrior Battle Captain myself on my cell phone and let him know what's happening," I added.

That obviously made Cougar 13 feel better.

"Roger that, EOD 6," came the belated reply.

Being a captain had occasional advantages, and Castleman had not wasted the time I bought him. While I kept us from being abandoned, our robot had placed an explosive-and-water mix near the wires connecting the battery to the blasting cap, and was reloaded back in our truck.

"Fire in the Hole!" *Booom!* The device came apart and scattered across the bridge, alerting half of Kirkuk to our presence.

The small-arms fire exchanges increased between Bayonet 23 and the gunmen on the near bank as we made the lonely drive back up the bridge to investigate the dismembered device. Quickly pieces and parts were loaded in our truck: a possible fingerprint here, a telltale wire knot there. I grabbed the mortar shell, a massive turkey leg, five pounds of explosives encased in thirty-five pounds of steel, and dumped it unceremoniously in the back of the truck for future disposal. Castleman called on the radio to Bayonet 23, who could now finally cross the bridge, as we quickly lined up and left the angry crowds behind. The Colonel stared out the window.

Off we drove, our little five-truck convoy, through the twitching city, to a smoldering car, a burning market, a pile of bodies, screaming children, and a long, long night.

I read in my hometown newspaper that a local art gallery, the big one at the college, has a new exhibit. It's an antiwar piece, a mix of media that demonstrates how terrible conflict is. The paper says it's earnest and powerful and contains Truth. I decide to go.

The room is small. A video plays on the far wall, continuously scrolling a list of names. Names of our dead. Black bags hang on strings from the ceiling, like giant popcorn necklaces, filling half the room. Each bag is supposed to hold the name of a soldier. More names of our dead. There are a lot of bags.

The artist has a narrative posted on the wall, an explanation of the piece. It talks about the moral choice of being a soldier in war. It says soldiers, when confronted with the horrors of war, have to make a choice: To fight or not. To participate or not. Suicide, it says, is the only moral choice.

The Crazy feeling explodes in my chest and makes my head spin. I start to shake.

Maybe it's right. Maybe I've made the wrong choice all along. I know what I did. I know what I wanted to do.

And now it's caught up with me. I can't live like this.

Not my whole life. Not the rest of my life like this. With the Crazy.

Something has to change.

It has to end.

v | *The Day of Six VBIEDs*

I DON'T REMEMBER when we realized there were six. Perhaps we should have expected it, after hitting the EFP Factory That Wasn't the day before. But I was tired, so tired, gorging on coffee from my enormous desert-camouflaged travel mug simply to stay awake, and when the first call came in, I sent off a team like it was any other event, any other bag or suspicious pile of trash along any highway in Iraq.

But it wasn't. Five minutes later there was another call. And then another. We stepped outside of the HAS, and saw three pillars of black smoke rising from the center of the city. A fourth pillar appeared before we ran inside to answer the phone again. Within fifteen minutes there were six. Six car bombs, attacking locations throughout the city. Later we called it the Day of Six VBIEDs.

Castleman took the first team to the local Patriotic Union of Kurdistan office, the site of the first attack, while I left with the second team five minutes later. Together we leapfrogged from blast site to blast site, from smoke cloud to smoke cloud. Count the bodies, collect the evidence, clear the scene, destroy leftover hazards. Mostly count the bodies.

Ewbank, Mitchell, Crisp, and I headed to the second call, to the Kurdish day care for crippled children. That sounds fake, right? Like I just made that up? Like I picked the stereotype of the most horrific possible target of a suicide car bomb? If only. Just before nine o'clock in the morning, a purple Opel detonated in the outdoor play area after ramming through the mud courtyard wall. We arrived to comb through the aftermath.

There was little to see at the day care. A smoking and charred black skeleton of a car, an engine block thrown through a crumbling home. The screaming crowds that would accompany us the rest of the day were thinning quickly, having already carried off the biggest portions of the victims. Two mangy feral dogs chewed on the little that was left. Four more car bombs to get to. We quickly pressed on.

Jimbo and I are running along the secluded creek-side path, past heaps of winter flotsam, tree-trunk strainers and rocky curves, a gray chilly winter day in eastern Washington. Jimbo and I are civilian trainers together, always on the road, EOD unit to EOD unit, a blur of travel and teaching. I'm running down the Crazy, and Jimbo obliges me as a running partner. But today my knee is screaming, and my lungs are ragged, and I can't keep up a pace that tamps the Crazy down. So Jimbo runs on ahead, but Ricky is on the trip too, and he hangs back and keeps me moving, even if it's at a slower gait.

"How far you wanna run today?" Ricky asks.

"I want to go my full six miles. Do a 10K. Can you do it?" I respond, huffing and wincing. My knee won't stop protesting, but at least the pain fully occupies my mind.

"I'd like to finish the whole thing. I hope we have time," Ricky answers.

Ricky and I press on, around brown rolling hills and under

old abandoned railroads, following the river swollen with the spring thaw. But I've developed a limp that is throwing off my stride, no matter how I ignore the pain in the ligament on the outside of my knee. Soon my pace slows again, and Ricky is checking his watch.

"If we're going to get back in time, before it gets dark, we need to turn around," Ricky says.

I protest, but he's right, and reluctantly we turn back toward the hotel. Jimbo catches us on the way back, and we all finish the last leg together as the sunset turns deep purple, the street-lights coming on in bunches. Jimbo ran the full 10K we had mapped out before, and tells us of a waterfall he saw around a bend we never made it to, another mile past where we had to turn around. It sounds great, but Ricky and I never do make it all the way to see it ourselves.

They had already started screaming before we arrived. It continued the entire time we worked. It probably continued after we left.

More than a scream. A high-pitched shriek, and sob, and vomit, and a scream again.

Men usually formed the bulk of the crowds that gathered spontaneously at bombings and attacks, huddled in dress clothes and leather loafers, faces full of concern and suspicion. This crowd was different from the moment we arrived. There was a small group of women across the narrow street from the crater formed by the second car bomb; in their screams they created a din that rivaled any shouts and chants from any male throng I had ever heard. And because there were women, they brought their children, crying an echo of their mothers' wail. Small children, barefoot in the sewage and blood. And one boy, barely a teenager, who stared at our armored truck as we arrived with overtly hot contempt and hatred. The crowds of men never looked you in the eye, even if you spoke to them. But this boy's direct gaze burned through the armored glass between us. His eyes never left me, never wavered, never stopped boring through Kevlar and steel and flesh to see what, if anything, lay beneath.

Even the meager trees were blackened by the enormous blast that felled half a city block. Somehow the target, a police colonel and Kurdish commander of the city's SWAT team, managed to survive. He was still inside his home when the suicide bomber drove the explosive-laden car into his drive-way. His bodyguards, who had come that morning to pick him up and take him to work, were standing in the driveway next to the official police vehicle. I never did find much of it. We found the entrails of the bodyguards on the roof of a home a quarter mile away.

The foot didn't sit in the box. Not yet.

The Iraqi Police who arrived before us made no pretense of holding back the crowds, swelled and frantic, pouring over the scene, collecting pieces of loved ones and already mourning the dead. What evidence could we possibly find in the chaos? My frustration grew as the shell of the suicide bomber's car was loaded on a tow-truck bed before we had a chance to examine it. Iraqi policemen brought us arms and hands, ges-turing and talking hysterically, but with no terp around we understood little. The colonel himself had already left for the main police station to plan a reprisal against the Arab faction that produced the suicide bombers. And through it all, the women never stopped screaming, never stopped chanting, never stopped their piercing clamor.

Why are we even here, I thought, if hundreds have already

tromped through, swept up, recovered, snatched, or spirited away whatever tiny shreds of evidence may have been available? Why do I care who the bomber was? Why do I care what explosives he used? What trigger? What car, and where it was stolen from? If they don't care, why should I?

The boy continued to stare, and the women continued to shriek, and my anger grew with the volume of their grief. Did they think I liked wading knee-deep through their former cousins, sons, brothers, children? Did they not see that I was trying to help? But every move the crowd made set me back another half step, an accumulation of a thousand ingratitudes. The removal of a speck of explosive residue here, the grabbing of the bomber's license plate there. The mob swarmed like ants anywhere we had to work. Why did they have to make an awful job next to impossible?

And will no one shut these women up! The screams never abated, seared through my earplugs, and branded my brain.

I noted my rifle again, heavy in my hand. I can shut these women up. If no one else will do it, if the Iraqi Police won't move them on, get them home, then I can stop the screaming.

I put my right thumb on the safety, and my finger on the trigger.

I could do it. There are only, what, five or six? I could kill five or six women to stop the shrieking. It would be worth it, to stop this migraine tearing my skull apart, to stop the mindless wailing and gnashing.

I fantasized about it. My finger got twitchy in anticipation as the adrenaline began to flow. I couldn't take my eyes off them now, heads modestly veiled, hands covering their wrinkled faces stained with tears. Still the screaming did not stop.

The teenage boy stared through me, and saw nothing inside. I stared back at the women, and flipped my rifle off Safe. I

could do this. I am capable of it. I can end this insolent screaming now.

"Come on, Captain, let's go," said Ewbank. "There ain't shit
here to find. And anyway, we got another call. They found a car
bomb that didn't go off. Let's di di mau."

There are two of me now. The logical one watches the Crazy
one.

The Crazy one is living the life. The Crazy one wakes up,
and wonders if today I will be Crazy. And the answer is always
yes.

The Crazy one dresses the kids, packs lunches, drives them
to school. The Crazy one showers, eats, cleans. The Crazy one
flies to work, trains soldiers, flies home. The Crazy one sleeps
next to my wife, goes to hockey practice, checks math home-
work. The Crazy one runs and runs and runs. The Crazy one
is always Crazy.

But the logical one can step back and observe. The logical
one watches, waits, comments. The logical one knows there is
another way. Knows that this life is not a life. Knows I used to
enjoy things, even some of the things I'm doing now. Knows
that there must be a cure for the Crazy. Knows that the Crazy
must not always be, simply because it is right now, at this
moment. There was a time before the Crazy. The logical one
knows there must be a time after.

But the logical one is powerless, trapped, a shade looking
over the shoulder of the Crazy one frantically whirling. It can
only watch, as my chest fills, and my stomach boils, and my
head comes off, and I simply endure from minute to minute.

It took the Kurds just a few minutes to figure out what was going on. But once they did, they started fighting back as ruthlessly as they had for thousands of years. The Kurds and Arabs hate each other more than most can fathom, and the retaliations began before the car-bomb attack had even ended. On the Day of Six VBIEDs, five car bombs went off. One did not. The Kurds shot the sixth driver in the temple as he approached the final target. That failed bomber sat now in the gray Japanese car a hundred yards in front of me, slumped but upright, blood splattered across the interior driver's window, an intact device under the hatchback ready to blow. A bomb for us to clear, a building and family that would not be destroyed today. It was the only VBIED on the entire tour that we would safe before it detonated.

Mitchell drove the robot down to the car bomb and verified what the Kurds had told us. A dead bomber in the front seat, a suicide switch wrapped around the automatic transmission lever next to the emergency brake, electrical wires running to the car battery, a pile of propane tanks filled with homemade bang, primed with wads of gooey plastic explosives and held together with black electrical tape in the rear cargo compartment.

Crisp and I went to the back of the Humvee to get an explosive tool for the robot to drag down and place under the car. I lit another cigarette; smoking was the least dangerous thing I did all day.

"Which one do you think Ewbank wants?" asked Crisp.

"I guarantee it'll be the Boot Banger," I answered.

Sidney Alford, eccentric British inventor and demolitions man, developed the Boot Banger in the mid 1980s to take apart IRA car bombs in Northern Ireland. A boxy briefcase-sized mix of explosives and water, Boot Bangers remove everything from the trunk of a car, usually by turning the vehicle inside out. To the uninitiated a harmless-looking black plastic box, like an overgrown piece of toy luggage, the Boot Banger sandwiched layers of water and explosive to great effect. We had meticulously prepped the tool back at the HAS, carefully slicing the quarter-inch-thick sheets of explosive to fit. All we needed to do was add water and cap in.

The crowd around us predictably began to grow, but this time, instead of a pressing mob or wailing women, our company was AK-47-armed Kurdish *peshmerga,* tribal militia determined to secure their homes and exact revenge. The radio crackled with a report of multiple black vans of masked gunmen, sporting rocket-propelled grenades, on their way to our location. Our terp had a hurried conversation with the *pesh* commander, gesturing to the west and north. Soon the gunmen began shouting and running off together toward the heart of the city. Gunfire erupted in the distance, and I never saw a black van.

The robot ripped the suicide switch off the gear shift and then slid the Boot Banger in flat beneath the hatch, on the ground between the pavement and undercarriage. Ewbank popped the initiator, the tool exploded, and propane tanks and detonating cord flew into the air, ripped free by the expelling force of the water jet. In minutes it was safe enough to head down to the car, dismantle the rest of the bomb by hand, and inspect the Kurdish handiwork.

I leaned in the passenger side, collecting pieces of evidence, and examined the body seated behind the steering wheel, still perfectly intact, so focused is the Boot Banger's effect. The thwarted suicide bomber's head leaned to the side, covered in a fine layer of dust kicked up from our explosive clearing charge. His eyelashes were dirty; that's how I knew he was dead. If he were alive, that layer of dust would tickle, and he would have brushed off his eyelids and nose. But the dust had settled and did not irritate. Nothing would spur this fleshbag to move again, even the flies now coming in.

I stared at the hole in his skull. It was dark, empty. His brain had been pushed in, leaked out the exit wound on the other side, and I couldn't see it from this angle. A black hole in his skull, just above the temple, the diameter of my index finger.

I wanted to put my finger inside of it.

I am alone in my full bed. Alone with the Crazy, in the bed where the spiders crawl out of my head and the ceiling presses down to crush me. Always bubbling, always boiling, always intolerable, the Crazy feeling swells me to bursting again. I'm crawling out of my skin. It's been three and a half months now. The Crazy hasn't let up yet.

My wife rolls over and pretends to be asleep. We have gone to bed without speaking. Again. She is wearing a yellow T-shirt as a nightgown, the words "Kirkuk, Iraq" emblazoned across the front in bold black letters. You get a T-shirt for everything now. Running a race. Opening a bank account. Giving blood. Elbowing your neighbor to catch a shot from a pop-gun at a minor-league baseball game. I even have one for fighting the Battle Creek forest fire in South Dakota. A T-shirt for a forest fire. Why not one for fighting a war?

My wife is alone in our full bed too. Her husband, the father of her children, never came back from Iraq. When I deployed the first time she asked her grandmother for advice. Her grandfather served in Africa and Europe in World War II. Her grandmother would know what to do.

"How do I live with him being gone? How do I help him when he comes home?" my wife asked.

"He won't come home," her grandmother answered. "The war will kill him one way or the other. I hope for you that he dies while he is there. Otherwise the war will kill him at home. With you."

My wife's grandfather died of a heart attack on the living-room floor, long before she was born. It took a decade or two for World War II to kill him. When would my war kill me?

My wife wasn't prepared to sit and wait for my collapse. She considered it a gift, grace from above, that I got fired and sent home early from Balad. No way I could tempt fate twice and emerge unscathed. Better to consider me dead the day I got on the plane for Kirkuk. Her mental preparation was validated; as far as she could tell, I came home Crazy. She tells me that I didn't laugh, not once, for an entire year after I got back. Crazy was like dead for her.

I know she's strong enough to handle it. The girl I met our senior year, straight A's, future emergency-room nurse, college swim team, was strong enough. Strong enough to deal with my deployments and time away. Strong enough to wait for the knock on the door while watching the carnage on the evening news. Strong enough to deal with a Crazy husband. Strong enough to raise our sons by herself. Strong enough, if called upon, to open the letter I wrote before I left, to be read to our boys if I came home in a bag, explaining why their father went away to die in some city they can't find on a map. To this day that letter sits in a small safe, inches away from where I now sit and type. It sits in that safe unopened and undiscarded because I don't remember what I wrote and I can't bear to look now to find out. But my wife could have done it. She's strong enough. She's not scared of the soft sand.

So if she needs to cry herself to sleep next to me in bed, then she just needs to cry. If she needs to not speak, then she will stay silent. If she needs to replan her life to support four sons and a couch-ridden Crazy husband, then she will do what she needs to do. She can hack it. She's just going to have to. What can I do about it now, lying here in bed alone? I'm Crazy.

Our Marriage Counselor, fat and sweaty, fingers intertwined and resting on the shelf of his enormous stomach, diagnosed the situation.

"Why is the war still in your house?" he huffed. "Get it out of your bed."

Too late. We are in a bed full of rifles and helicopters and twitching eyes and Kermit's blue skin and the foot in the box. My wife sleeps next to the shade of a dead man every night.

I sleep alone, with the Crazy. And its gray spidery fingers take the top of my head off to eat my brain and heart from the inside out every night as I stare at the ceiling in my solitary bed.

"We should ID this motherfucker. Where are the weapons intel guys?" asked Ewbank.

We had cleared out the last of the physical evidence from the car bomb and were prepping the homemade explosive-filled propane tanks for demolition. Incoming bullets zipped and pinged off our trucks, *snicker-snack* off the crumbling concrete houses. The dead bomber with the hole in his head still sat in the front seat.

"They're on another car bomb now with Castleman's team," I replied. "Should I call them to get them over here?"

"Nah, we don't have time. Do we have a fingerprint kit in the truck?" asked Ewbank.

"I don't think so. Weapons intel has them all."

"Did we check his wallet at least?"

"Didn't have one. I bet the Kurds grabbed it before we got here."

"Well, we need something for this asshole," said Ewbank, and thought a minute, finger to his lips.

"You guys could cut off his fingers and take them with you," suggested a voice from above. It was the turret gunner from a nearby security Humvee, obviously eavesdropping on our conversation. The barrel of his short belt-fed machine gun was visibly warm from returning the sporadic incoming fire that had harassed us all afternoon, a faint whisper of smoke slipping from the bore. The kid smiled and looked proud of himself for having such a good idea. Thinking outside of the box.

I considered.

"Probably not a good idea. We don't have a good way to keep them from rotting on the way to central processing in Baghdad."

"Yeah, good point. Well, one more unidentified suicide bomber in this world won't hurt much. Let's pack up and go," said Ewbank.

We blew the propane tanks in a nearby field where they wouldn't hurt anyone or anything. The Kurds must have dragged off the body. I don't know. We left it and the car where they lay.

Two months later we had a Day of Five VBIEDs. But by that time I was numb, my brain atingle, and I have no memory of it at all.

Terrorism and modern war are only possible in their current form because of the scientific application of high explosives. Poor pale cousins of these dark riders appeared before, but the true potential for human cruelty was only discovered on a grand scale once man could kill tens or hundreds or thousands in one act, rather than take single lives with a spear or a club.

Explosives being the key ingredient in the conflict, it would seem logical that those that neutralize said explosives would play a pivotal role. Such logic, however, is wrong. Most state-employed weapons are designed to detonate immediately at their target, and it is only an unintended consequence that unexploded munitions would be present on the battlefield. Civil War cannonballs, Great War artillery shells and mortars, World War II rockets and flak, Vietnam War anti-aircraft missiles and hand grenades were all meant to kill immediately. It is only when terrorism and modern war are mixed, one side choosing to integrate fear into its strategic plan, that the neutralizer comes to prominence. Because then the bomb technician is not so much a disposer of waste as a bringer of calm, a foil to the fundamental method by which your enemy wishes to wage war.

Twice in modern war has the bomb technician found himself a historic fulcrum. Our first chance we won. The second, we failed before we started.

Nazi Germany swept up the Poles, Belgians, Dutch, and French in a tidal wave that crashed on the high white cliffs of the British Isles. To put another notch in Hitler's belt, the Luftwaffe needed to defeat two foes: the pesky insects buzzing around the ears of their expansive bomber formations, and the stout hearts of the British people. The first they attacked with Messerschmitts. The second they attacked with fire bombs and V rockets in the Blitz.

Germany knew the factories of Britain, Canada, and the United States would have been able to perpetually provide sufficient airplanes and pilots. Thus the first foe would only fall if the second failed first. The real battle lay with the will of the

British people to endure, contingent in large measure on the efforts of the Unexploded Bomb (UXB) brigades.

Not every bomb dropped is going to detonate. Some will malfunction, no matter the precision of the engineering or mechanical specifications. So when German bombs dropped on London neighborhoods but did not detonate, someone had to go clear them. The UXB squads combed through craters and crushed buildings.

Unfortunately, German ingenuity foresaw this eventuality and spotted an opportunity. If a bomb could be dropped with a timer, so that it would hit the ground and not detonate, and by all accounts appear to be a dud, then someone would come to dispose of it. But if the bomb fuze timer was set properly, it could detonate later, surrounded then by men clearing it by hand. The Germans developed such timers in the 1930s, and sold them to Franco's Spain, where they worked to great effect and delight. This strategy worked the first time in Britain. And probably the second. But soon, the British awoke to the danger, and the bomb technician was born.

Thus a game of cat and mouse developed, each side now fully engaged in the deadly contest before them. British UXB squads learned the inner workings of German timing systems, and disarmed them prior to detonation. German fuze builders then incorporated antitamper features, anti-withdrawal snares, to spoil the new safing methods. The British developed their tactics on the fly, on the battlefield, sending one technician to the bomb with hand tools—hammers, screwdrivers, and hand-crank drills—while the rest of the team stayed back and made meticulous notes. They performed one step at a time, loosened one screw at a time, and detailed each success and failure. If drilling to the left of the fuze caused it to detonate yesterday, then they drilled to the right today, writing a book of procedures to thwart each German re-engineer.

UXB teams cleared the bombs. The fire brigades stopped the inferno. The British people did not yield. The bomb technician gave his full measure, and ultimately shifted the strategic direction of the war.

In Iraq, however, our second opportunity, we saw the challenge before us, and declined to meet it.

As American and British divisions raced over the Kuwaiti border, entering Basra, Kut, and Najaf on the way to Baghdad and beyond, soldiers discovered unguarded and open ammunition bunkers, huge complexes of high-explosive artillery rounds, aircraft bombs, mines, and guided missiles. Instead of securing and destroying those depots, we left them as we found them, moving on to richer targets and swift regime change. In some locations we tested for biological and chemical weapons, finding little other than old rusting hulks, cracked bombs, and hollow rocket warheads. In others, we nabbed the few pieces with technical intelligence value and shipped them back to the United States. Most we left to rot in the open, exposed, vulnerable, not forgotten but simply dismissed as unimportant.

By the end of the year, those ammunition bunkers were empty, stripped clean by Iraqi militants and redistributed for us to dispose of one by one, hidden by the side of the road.

"Let me tell ya something," the old Chief said to the young officers.

"Are ya ready," the Chief asked, "because I'm going to blow your fuckin' minds."

The Chief had been in EOD longer than I had been alive.

I was ready for any insight, any bits of wisdom, as I sat in the nighttime darkness by the man-made lake outside of the Task Force headquarters. A couple of my fellow EOD commanders and I were meeting at the sprawling base west of Baghdad for a little redirection from higher. The Chief was the informal portion of that.

We waited. The Chief considered his dark cigar, held gently in his dark hand.

"IEDs are dope," the Chief said. "They're nuthin' but fuckin' dope. You think you're saving the day clearing out that IED? You're just snatchin' the user. You think you're getting ahead taking down the weapons caches? Those are just the sellers. We could wax guys for smokin' and sellin' dope for the next thirty years, and there would always be more dope. We could catch 'em bringing it across the border, and there will always be more dope. There is so much dope all over this country, we'll never find it all. And even if we do, if they still want it, they'll grow it themselves. That's the thing about dope. There's always more."

We sat in dejected silence for a moment. The Chief took another puff on his cigar, cherry-red tip bright in the desert night.

"Well, then, what do we do?" I asked, for the group.

"You can only do two things," said the Chief. "The first is to try to get them to not want dope anymore. The problem is, as long as we're here, everybody wants dope, and they always will."

"So what's the second thing, then, if the first won't work?" I asked.

"Get everybody's ass home in one motherfuckin' piece," the Chief replied, deadly serious. "You gotta take care of everyone and get them home to Mamma. It takes five things to live through Iraq. Luck, training, luck, equipment, and luck. Say your prayers every night before you go to bed, kiss that fuckin' rosary you got, and maybe we'll all get home to drink some beer at the fuckin' strip club before all this shit's over."

The first time I met Albietz he was covered in blood. Not his own, but I didn't know that yet.

Albietz and Meadows and Roy were stuck at Bernstein, a lonely outpost south of Kirkuk. Spartan Bernstein existed to watch over the town of Tuz, a sleepy *ville* that vacillated between bouts of subsurface tension and extreme violence. As the EOD team there fought boredom and sleep loss in uncertain quantities, I had them come back to the main base every so often for a good meal, a hot shower, and an explosives resupply.

The attack occurred on one such trip. A heavily armed convoy of Humvees doesn't snake north on the deserted highway from Tuz very often. There is only one wide, main route through the sprawling city of Kirkuk when approaching from the south. There is no way to prevent a solitary spotter down in Tuz from calling his cousin in an IED cell operating up in the city. It is too simple to predict when and where the convoy will pass a certain street corner, chosen for its hidden infiltration and escape routes. It is too easy to cut through our armor with an array of EFPs.

The detonation hit the Humvee directly in front of Albietz, Roy, and Meadows. The front concave plate of each EFP melted into a hot comet of molten copper, a heavy center mass trailing burning globs, morphed by the force of the densely packed explosive propelling it. One dirty slug entered the rear passenger door, cut through three legs, and then splattered and ricocheted inside the compartment of the armored truck.

The EOD team responded first, being the first to see the attack and quickest to the scene. Roy swept for secondary devices that might be lying in wait to kill soldiers providing first aid. Albietz waded into a red wet hell and began to apply tourniquets around thighs, above where knees used to be. The soldier closest to the door lost two legs, the gunner lost one. The femoral artery that runs down the interior of each meaty leg can pump a fire hose of blood when there is a healthy heart of a vibrant twenty-year-old involved. Albietz bathed in it as he worked.

I knew none of this when Meadows, Roy, and Albietz arrived at the HAS, our compound on the FOB. Albietz came in first; silent, pallid, bald head splotchy and brown. I was in the ops center, writing another report, reviewing another report, drinking another cup of coffee to compensate for the late mission the night before. I offhandedly greeted the presence I felt, a brown-and-gray-camouflaged haze in my peripheral vision, without looking up.

Albietz said nothing. He stumbled a bit at the front of the desk.

Griffin noticed something was wrong first. He jumped up from the ops center where he was working, waiting for a call, and grabbed Albietz as he started to sway. I finally looked up to see Albietz reaching for the wall to steady himself, still girded in his body armor, leaning on his rifle. He was not camouflaged in brown and gray. He was camouflaged in gray but drenched in blood now dried brown, splattered across his vest, arms, face. Only deep white patches around his eyes were spared, where his sunglasses had caught the spray instead.

I went with another crew to check out the Humvee that had been hit. It had been towed to the FOB motor pool, and was awaiting our inspection. Blood still pooled in the foot well of the backseat; it hadn't yet evaporated in the desert heat. The telltale copper of the EFP slug plated the mouth of the Humvee's entrance wound and was flecked around the interior of the cab, embedded in the back wall, around the gunner's harness and port. The mortuary team hadn't made it to the Humvee yet; there was still a boot containing its proper appendage tossed in one corner. I closed the door and left after only a moment or two. There was nothing else to learn here, and I couldn't take the smell.

I didn't know Albietz before that day, before I met him for the first time covered in blood that wasn't his. I hugged him and put him in the shower, unable to do anything more.

The naïve excitement of combat lasted little longer than a month. Every day I tried to appreciate living my dream, and every day I failed. The exhaustion set in, and I walked through the war in a haze.

Up too early in the morning, after a restless night of fever dreams, phone calls, and rockets impacting the base. Cold cereal at my plywood desk, in front of my computer, catching up on intelligence reports that came in overnight. And then the wait for a call: a mission, an assault, a car-bomb detonation in the city, the news that someone died. The mission comes, you go and return, and then the waiting resumes.

The lunches melded into dinners that all tasted the same. The days turned into weeks, and weeks into months. They became a blur of cigarettes and explosions, situation-report deadlines and bloody pieces of children, bone-weary exhaustion and black, black coffee.

And in relief, shoehorned awkwardly in between, phone calls once a week home to my wife to chat, about a son's failed math test, a child's anxiety at day care. Her voice was clipped and short. Because she was sick of being lonely, sick of my being gone? Or because she had finally given up and found someone else to warm her bed?

Don't be scared of the soft sand! This is where I want to be. This is where I need to be. I chose this. Love it! Appreciate it! You'll miss it when it's gone.

How do you appreciate dismantled children?

The war didn't pause for an answer.

"Can you believe they pay us to drive around this country and blow things up? It's like the whole place is one giant demolitions range!" gushed Hodge, newly arrived and fresh off the plane, at the chow hall one afternoon, over a lunch of ash and ice cream. His buzz hadn't worn off yet.

"Yes, I can," answered Keener. He lost his buzz the first time he stepped in something human, and couldn't tell what it was.

"Let's go before the afternoon VBIEDs," I mumbled. We picked up our trays, dropped them with the dishwashers, and, walking outside, watched smoke rise from downtown in the distance. The call would come in before we got back to our compound.

I am sitting in my Old Counselor's tiny office at the VA hospital in Buffalo. She looks sad. And concerned. She always looks concerned.

I've just related how the Crazy feeling expands when I stand in line at McDonald's. And in airports. Definitely alone in airports. In an unknown crowd, the need to move away. . . .

The Crazy feeling hasn't stopped since that day, the day I went Crazy. It's been four months now. It never gets better; it never goes away. But it does get worse.

My Old Counselor is scribbling on her pad as I am telling the story of trying to get some lunch while out on the road on a job in Texas. "Triggers," she writes on the off-green top-bound spiral legal pad. What does "triggers" mean? I doubt she is talking about the one on the rifle I have strapped to my chest, snugged up tight to my right shoulder.

"I wasn't sure before," she says, "but I am now."

"What are you sure of?" I ask. I fidget with my flip-flops. I have a bad feeling I know the answer.

"You have PTSD," she says.

Fuck. I am Crazy.

VI | *Kermit*

KERMIT DIED IN December, the December after I got back from Kirkuk, the December I didn't laugh, several Decembers before I went Crazy. Looking back on it now, how our paths bent together, met, and then diverged again, each following the other's trail in a tragic mirror, I see that there were too many coincidences for Fate to have allowed our relationship to turn out well.

Captain Kermit O. Evans was from the little town of Hollandale in western Mississippi. I never made it to that town for the memorial service, though now I wish I had. I was already going to four funerals and memorial services for Kermit, so I skipped the fifth. I didn't want to endure a fifth. I was too tired to go. How silly that sounds now.

I met Kermit while he was training to become an EOD technician in Florida and I was rotting away for a month at a useless professional development course for officers, a knife-and-fork school in Montgomery, Alabama. We had dinner at a bad chain restaurant, sat in the bar, and spent the entirety of our mealtime discussion on his new world as a bomb technician. I, the old experienced veteran, passing on wisdom to the new guy.

Kermit and I met because he was taking over command of my EOD unit in New Mexico. Despite my recent firing in Balad, I was being reassigned to Nellis, a bigger unit at a bigger base, in Las Vegas. Kermit was headed to Cannon after finishing up his EOD training, but had come from an engineering job at Nellis previously. We were swapping bases. The officer who saw past my checkered history and pulled the strings to get me the Nellis job also put in a good word to get Kermit a slot at EOD school. Chance and a couple of phone calls brought us to the same town at the same time. He told me places to buy a house in Vegas. I told him when his new unit was headed back to Iraq. Kermit was very earnest and excited. He was always earnest and excited, often to the delight of those around him. I do not delight easily; I saw a naïve black kid who was taking over my job and who had no idea what he was getting himself into.

We ate, I drank a beer, we wished each other well, and our paths, briefly together, diverged once again. But Fate was not done. Fate would lead us back together and tie us in knots, but not on this side of Heaven; that dinner was the first and only time I saw Kermit alive.

I get the call from my boss, the commander of my squadron. It's on my home phone. Odd, since my commander usually calls on the smart phone given to me for that exact purpose. And it's late on a Sunday, after dinner. Also odd.

"Do you know a Kermit Evans?" my boss asks.

"Sure. He took over for me at Cannon. He's in Iraq now, I think, doing that weapons intel job."

"He's missing," my boss says.

"Missing how?" I ask.

"Missing as in his helicopter went down over the Haditha Dam and they can't find his body. Do you know Perneatha, his wife?"

"No, we've never met."

"Perneatha moved back home to Las Vegas while Kermit went to Iraq," my boss says. "They live a couple blocks from you. You're the Family Liaison Officer now—have your blues on and meet me in the morning. We're going to tell her."

My boss hangs up. I keep holding the phone.

My wife comes up and asks what's wrong. "Kermit's dead, and I'm the FLO," I say. I've never done that before. I have no idea what to expect.

"This may be the most important thing I ever do in the military," I tell her, and I mean it. I go into the bedroom and iron my uniform. Shoes polished, pants crisp. The story of my last eight years, told in little scraps of colored silk, endlessly straightened until perfect. I shine and shine and shine my Crab.

The next morning I meet my boss, who is also in blues, and we go get the Chaplain. Much discussion takes place about when to go to Perneatha's house. What time is best to tell a wife her husband is missing? It should not be too early in the morning, or one may rudely wake the wife, or catch her before she has gotten ready for the day. At the same time it can't be too late in the day. If you wait until noon, the wife will ask what took you so long, especially if it becomes clear her husband has been missing for some time. We go mid-morning. We don't know what else to do. This feeling pervades.

My boss says he will go in alone, and the Chaplain and I should wait. He doesn't want to overwhelm Perneatha. This is his job, the notification—we have other jobs later. We park in one of the ubiquitous Las Vegas cul-de-sacs. My boss approaches the door and does the unthinkable. The Chaplain and I wait in the car. The Chaplain makes small talk. He does death all the time. I'm the newbie to this version.

Later the door opens and we go in. Perneatha is sitting on the couch, calm, composed and put together, making phone calls, informing the family. Kermit Junior runs around the house in his diaper, barely a year old and excited by the visitors and entertainment. Perneatha asks questions. Why haven't they found him yet? Do you think he is dead? What is the chance he is not dead? Can you swim with body armor on? When will we know more? We have no good answers.

Family begins to arrive. Perneatha's sister lives in Las Vegas as well, and is at the house in a flash. Aunts and women from church arrive soon after. I never do figure out all the relations, but the house fills quickly. With nothing to do but wait for news, a routine sets in. The women cook: greens, chicken, biscuits. Kermit Junior runs around the living room while everyone watches. Perneatha chases him and smiles brave smiles. I sit on the couch. The foot sits in a box in the corner.

We find out later what happened to Kermit. He was based in Baghdad, but was traveling around Iraq, visiting the men and women who worked for him. Out west in Anbar, Kermit had loaded up on a CH-46 to fly to his next FOB. He was last in a line of three guys trying to fly Space A—meaning he would pack on at the end to fill any sliver of open room. On this bird only one seat was available, and the two Marines in front of him wanted to fly together. Kermit noted his good luck and skipped ahead to take the last seat.

After all scheduled passengers were aboard, Kermit was waved on by the flight engineer. When you load in the back of a chopper, you listen to the engineer without question. The bird comes in fast and loud, and you do a quick hot transfer. Two lines of buffeted men and women file out of the back and are dismissively waved to the side. You stand in line, loaded up with your body armor, pack, and weapon, and await the signal from the engineer in the back to move up. Kermit loaded up the same way I did a hundred times: into the back, to the side, file to a jump seat, the bird lifting off in seconds and then hurtling through space over a uniformly tan desert.

Except this time, Kermit's bird had a problem.

There are always problems when flying, though it is safer than driving. We stuffed our armored Humvees full of every piece of gear and article of faith we could find. C4 and TNT, plus commandeered enemy Semtex and PE4. Blasting caps, electric and non, and time fuze, shock tube, and radio systems to ignite them. Rolls of det cord and water tools of every description: Bottlers, Maxi-candles, EXIT charges, Boot Bangers, and modified Gatorade bottles, snuck out of the chow hall in bulk and surgically altered with a knife and electrical tape to accept a jerry-rigged explosive core. A bomb suit, bang sticks, one or two robots, their controllers, and extra batteries for both. A Barrett .50-cal sniper rifle, extra ammo, extra pistols, frag grenades, smoke grenades, and claymores when we could get them. Food and water for days. Always more water, to drink and for work, and empty bottles to piss in. Mounted between the driver and team chief we put the radio, the GPS, and the jammer, flickering its stream of reassurance.

The superstitious rituals of EOD school melded with resignation to Providence: never change your lucky underwear, never change your lucky pencil, never so much as touch the jammer that brought your ass home every day. I once nearly had to break up a fistfight when the poor contractor stopped by the HAS to swap out our old jammer for a newer model. I made sure the contractor left in peace, his eye unblackened, but only if he took the new jammer with him and promised to never come back.

On the outside of our Humvees we hung more talismans to ward off our fears. Antennas and turret mounts and storage bins for possibly hazardous IED components and pronged front-bumper kits to ram our way through civilian traffic. The infantry went a step further and mounted massive bolt-on armor kits to each door. An armored door already weighed more than two hundred pounds. Now each would be three hundred or more. I said no to the extra kits as well. Our first week at Kirkuk, Price dropped a wheel over the lip of a narrow canal road. The bank gave way and the Humvee slid in sideways, filling with water at the bottom of the sewage-filled channel. Our entire four-man team was trapped; wedged into that tiny box, no one had the strength or leverage to push a two-hundred-pound door open upward. The security team jumped on top of the sinking Humvee, and with three men lifting each door, extricated my brothers. If they had had the bolt-on kits, no amount of extra help would have been enough, and we would have lost four that day.

Steel beasts loaded with kit and dismounts, armored Humvees work better in packs. The trust was sacred between security and EOD team: outside the wire, they protected us from gunfire and grenades and kept us from getting lost; we protected them from IEDs and hidden danger and kept them from getting blown up. Only once did I ever drive alone, separated from our security. Within two klicks of our base at Balad, the FOB a dome of light on the horizon, our security allowed us to drive back on our own from an aborted mission. What could happen so close to home? Driving center of the road as fast as he could, Weston never saw the string of low highway barriers on the double-yellow stripe. It was just past twilight, too light for night-vision goggles and too dark to keep your headlights off, and we drove our armored truck at full speed into the awaiting concrete ram. Twelve thousand pounds of man and machine stopped in an instant. Stationed behind the driver, I flew forward into his seat and surrounding frame. My bifocal NVGs, mounted on my helmet, split in half on impact. Weston was saved when the plate in his vest absorbed the crushing steering wheel against his chest. The Humvee nosed in, and the front tires curled and bent, coming to rest on top of the hood. We were alone, without security, our mount a dead heap on the side of the road, put down through our carelessness. We radioed the FOB for help, and then waited in the dark for relief, guarding that armored truck and the millions of dollars' worth of classified equipment it contained. At that moment, jumping at every snap and pop and sound of distant gunfire, surrounded by hobgoblins and the shades of gunmen, I swore I'd never leave our convoy escort for any reason ever again.

Flying is safer than driving, but when you're nothing but helpless baggage, it wears at the nerves. People and cargo are loaded on together and shoehorned into stifling sweatboxes for the duration. Every bird has its quirks. Black Hawks are tiny—ten to twelve seats—and provide a unique intimacy with the side gunners and outside world. The "hurricane seat" on the starboard rear will fill your face with dust and grime, as the downdraft from the overhead rotor ripples and shakes your cheeks. I always begged for the hurricane seat because I had too many vivid memories of baking in Shithooks, Sherpas, and Hercs, desperate for a non-fuel-encrusted whiff of fresh air.

C-130 Hercules cargo planes made the milk run visiting FOBs in Iraq, and were a decent ride if you could get them. I learned to avoid the Aussies; while U.S. Air Force pilots dodge surface-to-air missiles by climbing as high as they can as fast as they can, the suicidal Aussies cling to the landscape to limit the time an enemy has to take aim and fire. The downside: the 150-degree air in the back never cools when you stay a hundred feet from the ground, skimming above the Baghdad palm trees and power lines for thirty minutes, waiting until you hit the outskirts of town and it's safe to climb.

The Marines are no better, flying at night and in the worst neighborhoods. On approach and landing one night at a postage stamp of an airfield, we started to take incoming fire. This is less obvious than one might think. With no windows or flight plan for reference, the cargo hold becomes a timeless vibrating barrel. The only indication of landing is an odd gravitational sensation as the pilot edges the nose down, banks to the left, points a wing tip toward the airfield below, and begins the corkscrew descent. The shaking increases alarmingly as your back presses into your seat and your heart rises into your throat. The engineers in the tail grab their night-vision goggles and take their positions in the sling seats at the two porthole-like back windows, hands around the flare-ejection triggers, looking for the hot-motor flashes of incoming heat-seeking missiles. Blinding-white flares are the only defense a wallowing C-130 has against smart and agile surface-to-air missiles. Small-arms fire from rifles, the tracers arcing across the sky, is pretty and ignored. They plink ineffectually off the bottom of the plane. Shoulder-fired missiles bring down birds like a Herc, and this is what my Marine flight engineers were searching for that night.

I only knew we were taking missile fire because the engineers began to thumb their buttons furiously, and suddenly daylight shone through their windows, lighting up the entire back of the aircraft. Seconds later we slammed onto the runway, jolted up and forward, and the engines screamed in reverse to bring the bird to an almost immediate stop. The ramp went down, in the middle of the runway where we had come to a halt, and the engineers screamed for everyone to get off. The pilot had called an emergency, audible only in the headsets of the flight crew, and everyone needed to get off the plane. Right. Fuck-ing. Now.

I grabbed my pack and rifle and ran off the plane into the waiting hot night oven. Down the ramp and onto the runway, where the engineers were already ahead of us, not waiting to see if the disoriented passengers could find their way. The air-field was completely blacked out, so as not to provide a tempt-ing target for rocket attacks, but incongruously there was light all over the runway: the flares and flare canisters kicked out of the plane by the engineers as we were only a few feet off the ground had ricocheted, angrily skipping down the tar-mac, burning all over the infield. I ran across the concrete and turned to look back at the aircraft, expecting to see engines on fire.

Instead, the pilot threw the emergency engine stop at that moment. The emergency cutoff kills all engine activity immediately, and everything flammable is jettisoned out the back. Like jet fuel. Four Allison AE2100D3 turboprop engines' worth of jet fuel came showering back, drenching me in liq-uid soot. I could taste the distinctive nauseating odor of JP-8 on my lips, in my eyes, in my ears. It soaked my uniform and oozed down my rifle like chocolate syrup. I stood on that runway as human tar paper, among the still-burning flares, in the desert night.

I'm sitting with Jimbo in another faceless airport, before dawn, drinking another cup of black coffee, waiting for another flight to I-can't-remember. Texas? North Carolina? It all blends together. If the city wasn't printed on the boarding pass, I wouldn't know where I was going. My life is a bad combination of rental-car shuttles, PowerPoints, identical chain restaurants, jet lag, hotel and airline reward programs, polo shirts, and explosives. The childlike joy of blowing things up is waning, and no longer makes up for the rest of the headaches.

Jimbo and John and Bill and I and the rest of the guys drove to the airport the way we always do: in a convoy, a line of unmarked SUVs and pickup trucks, fifteen miles per hour over the speed limit. We use handheld radios to coordinate while we drive, an unbroken column, unconsciously boxing out other drivers, bumper to bumper to keep civilian vehicles from cutting between. The lead truck blocks traffic when we change lanes on the highway, moving over and slowing suddenly to allow the rest of us to pass. Number two truck becomes point, former lead truck takes rear. The last man always runs the red light to stay together.

We never lose a vehicle. We don't talk about it. We don't have to.

I take another sip of coffee, look out the window at the awaiting aircraft, and then back over at Jim.

"Hey Jim—you know when you go down the Jetway to get on a plane, and you get that first stuffy whiff of the jet fuel? Do you think of Iraq every time?"

"Sure do, partner," Jim replies. "Hell, I think of Iraq any time I do anything."

But either conveyance, the Black Hawk or the C-130, is a blessing compared with the dreaded Chinook, called a Shithook by anyone who has ever flown in the back of one—slower, fatter, uglier, more uncomfortable and less tolerable; the Army cousin to Kermit's tragically doomed Marine bird. Even routine flights are miserable affairs, with inevitable yet still agonizing delays and hardships. You average one near-death experience per flight, and only some extraordinary bit of luck keeps you alive. It's a hell of a way to plan a mission. On a good night, you only do something like hit a mountainside, as we did once between Kirkuk and Tikrit. That low ridge of hills has lain between those two cities for thousands of years. Why our pilot flew too low on that dark night, slamming the front of the bird into the hill and throwing us into the air, I'll never know. The impenetrable blackness of the hazy night out the back ramp was suddenly filled with cliff and rock. I turned to the dirty contractor sitting next to me, pointed, and gave the "Did we really hit the fucking ground?" look. He nodded and shrugged back. What else can you do?

But accidentally hitting something is at least a stimulus, and a welcome relief from the worst rides. On my worst night the Shithook took the same route but stopped at every FOB and tiny airstrip in between. A two-hour trip stretched to twelve. The bird was loaded to capacity: forty-some unlucky Joes on the outside jump seats and three pallets of cargo squeezed down the middle. If you sit up front, you can get a tease of fresh breeze through the hatch past the M60 gunner's position. If you sit in the very back, you can suck in the main engine exhaust, which is at least moving air. If you are shoehorned in the middle, like me, you have the benefit of smelling all the exhaust but in a completely still bog of hot stale soup. You, your pack on your lap, and your rifle between your legs, all mashed into four cubic feet of space. Dudes on either side press against each hip and shoulder. The cargo pallet comes right up to your seat, so you have to lift your boots when it slides in, for fear of losing a foot. There it stays, eight inches from your nose, for twelve hours. It's four o'clock in the morning, you've been awake for a day and a half, and the air temperature is still well north of 110 degrees. Though you strain to turn your neck, there is little to see beyond indistinct forms and hazy silhouettes in the near darkness. So dehydrated are you that the sweat stopped running down your face hours ago, the only air to breathe is toxic exhaust, and you are vibrating in a tube of pain. If the heat and air don't make you nauseated, the swaying and shaking will. Don't worry; the only place to puke is on yourself, since you can't move anyway. It's as close to Hell as I can imagine on this earth.

You think about a lot of things on a flight like that. You can do nothing but think. I thought about my rifle. I counted every bullet in every magazine I had. Two hundred forty. I counted the number of motherfuckers trapping me inside that hellcan. I did the math. How many did I have to kill to get off? Twelve, blocking me from the back of the ramp. How many would try to stop me, and how many would try to join me? If the pilot heard shooting, he'd start to land, so the jump out the back might be survivable. My finger moved down to the Safe/Arm switch on my rifle. I could do it. This wasn't like being trapped on the ramp at O'Hare, a helpless civilian. I had a gun. I could make it all stop. The puking, the vibrating, the mashing. I flipped the switch on the rifle to Single, then to Auto, then back. Safe, Single, Auto, Single, Safe, Single, Auto. I could get off this fucking bird. Single. Safe. Single. Auto. I would do anything to make that flight stop. Single. Safe. Single. Anything. Auto. My thumb started to twitch. Single. I leaned my helmeted head up against the cargo in front of me, and took a noxious breath. Safe. Fuck me.

Kermit's chopper took off, turned to head out over Lake Qadisiyah behind the Haditha Dam, and immediately encountered trouble. What specific trouble is hard to say. As one might expect, the reports we got immediately after the incident did not match completely with later unclassified published accounts. In addition, any official Marine Corps safety report on the crash is either classified or unavailable. Reconstructing Kermit's last moments thus involve a mix of foggy memories from blast-shredded minds, educated guesses, and related experience.

What is clear, however, is that the main engine on the CH-46 failed almost immediately after takeoff. One eyewitness says the rear landing gear clipped the top of the dam on the way off the FOB, pitching the helo violently downward along the face of the concrete wall and toward the water. Whether this was a cause or a symptom of later trouble is unclear. In any case, rather than flying over the lake, the helicopter was now nosing toward it. When the motor on a CH-46 starts to shut down, there is no mistaking what is happening. It bucks and whines as the hydraulic pumps suddenly engage and then violently fall in pitch. A passenger hears that sound every time they land and the pilot kills the engine. There is no other sound like it. Hearing it in the air, above a body of water that you are hurtling toward, must have induced heart-bursting terror. Everyone on that bird must have known that the chopper was going down while over the lake.

The flight engineer, who normally mans the machine gun on the aft ramp where you enter and exit, started to evacuate everyone out the back of the aircraft. As the last passenger to board, Kermit was the first to be directed out, jumping into the lake as the chopper struggled. The bird partially recovered, flattening out over the water, and those stuck in the middle of the helo began streaming out the side hatches and gunner's port. Eventually the pilot and copilot, the last on board, somehow crabbed the damaged bird to the far shore and made a hard landing. Those two in the helicopter and ten of the rear passengers and crew survived with the help of responders who dove in the water to haul out frantic victims. One of those rescue swimmers was Murph, an EOD technician, Kermit's brother. He searched in the water in vain for the man he had just said good-bye to on the helo ramp moments before. All he ever found was Kermit's helmet and sunglasses.

Four of the passengers who jumped in the lake—two Marines, an Army Special Forces soldier, and Kermit—were sucked to the bottom by the weight of their gear and drowned.

I've imagined that moment in my head countless times. I can't believe Kermit would have jumped out of the helicopter on his own. As faux cargo, you never get in or out of the chopper unless directed by the engineer. Why didn't they delay their exit so they had time to remove their bulky armor and weapons? Or abandon the chopper in shallower water, closer to shore? What was Kermit thinking as he jumped, with his pack, rifle, and body armor still strapped on? Did he think he could wiggle out of it? Or was he just desperate to get out of the chopper, as I was over the plains of northern Iraq, and clawing to escape? Was he thinking at all? Did muscle memory take over? Did he know he didn't stand a chance? Did he know he was going to die?

The ritual was always the same. I put on my body armor first, a vest with attachments and additions, including side plates and ill-fitting shoulder coverings with extra straps. Then the rifle, with a three-point sling. The harness wraps around the left side of your neck, your right shoulder, and under the right armpit before reattaching to the rifle. It is not easy to slip off in normal circumstances; that's the point. Then a pack on top, shoulder straps on top of rifle sling, rifle sling over body armor closures. In ideal conditions, it takes sixty seconds to put on and thirty seconds to take off. In the water, after having just jumped out of a crashing helicopter, it takes minutes you don't have.

I'd have been pulled to the bottom under the weight of the life-saving armor. I'd have died with Kermit. When the divers found him in seventeen feet of water, his armored vest was on but open at the front, rifle sling hopelessly tangled about him.

It took a long time to find him, but eventually we get the news at Perneatha's house. An unrelenting series of memorial services, travel arrangements, and administrative tasks follows. Where is the body? When will it arrive in Delaware at the Air Force morgue? Who is escorting him? Will Kermit make it in time to his funeral? Was he bloated from being in the water, or could we have an open casket for everyone to say good-bye? When is the Las Vegas memorial? The Mississippi memorial? The New Mexico memorial? A wake before the Arlington funeral?

I feel awkward and helpless every day. You enter the house desperate to leave, eager for a task that takes you out again. What do you do for the long hours between news, between plans, between services? Your mind wanders. It's nearly Christmastime; have to go to the mall to buy the kids Christmas presents. Guilt. Who will buy Kermit Junior Christmas presents? The enormity of the event is overwhelming, and the mind seeks the mundane and familiar routine. You meet a family at the height of tragedy, at the height of their grief, bearing the worst possible news. Do you grieve with them? Is it rude not to? Is it rude of you to try? You don't share the family's history. You don't share their culture. You don't share their love of Kermit. Kermit was a fellow EOD technician, he is a brother, but he is not my husband, my father, my son. You walk the family through the painful steps of their grief, and then leave their life when only the very worst is over. You have a job to return to. They have a life to put back together. You pledge to keep in touch, but it is tentative. All I am to the family is a reminder of Kermit's death. All they are to me is the family I could not comfort.

I go home at night and clutch my children, confused and amazed it's not me lying in a morgue in Delaware.

The first memorial is in Las Vegas, for the friends Kermit had during his time stationed there, for the church Kermit and Perneatha attended, and the family that has flown in to be with her now. It is the first of five such services. In German Catholic Buffalo, where I grew up, you have a wake, a funeral, and coffee at Tim Hortons afterward. No one talks, everyone is fine, and life moves on. Perneatha and her family intend to grieve, in depth, regularly. More awkwardness.

For the Las Vegas memorial, several brothers make the trip from New Mexico. Kermit was their commander. Bill Hailer, Garet Vannes. Brothers I served with for two years during my time at Cannon. The scene comes full circle. I love them, and they love Kermit, and they're upset, but it feels off, unsettling. In the best of times it's strange to return to an old unit that you once commanded; "your guys" are no longer yours. Now my guys are mourning a man I don't really know. Would they have mourned me? I check my rifle. The foot sits in the box. I don't know why it wasn't me that fell out of a helicopter behind the Haditha Dam.

I only have a single part to play in the first service, and my part is small: the Last Roll Call and the Final Shot. After the readings, and the pastor's homily, and the songs, toward the end, you call a final roll call. I am the highest ranking EOD technician, and outranked Kermit, so it is my duty. You call the names of the members of the unit, as you would in any military formation. They respond back that they are present. It is a process that has happened every day in every military unit all over the world for thousands of years, but it takes on a final significance at a service such as this. The roll call is followed by a final shot, a last detonation, in honor of the deceased. It marks the closing chapter of his life as an EOD technician. Explosions mark all the significant events in the life of a bomb tech. Your first shot. Your first day on the bombing range. Your last call in theater. A shot at retirement. A shot at your funeral. How else would the Brotherhood mourn or mark the passing of time? It allows Kermit to rest.

I walk to the front of the base chapel, dress blues ironed, black shoes shined. I am followed by the roll-call formation. The rest of the memorial has been lively, festive even. A life was celebrated. Now the chapel is tempered, unsure. The formation stands in line in front of the altar, facing the assembled, at attention. I come to attention, left face. Absolute quiet fills the nave. I've never tried to stand straighter in my life.

"Senior Airman Kory!"

My voice fills the hall. I hear it ring. The response is immediate, full, proud.

"Here, sir!"

"Senior Airman Olguin!"

"Here, sir!"

"Staff Sergeant Leaverton!"

"Here, sir!"

"Technical Sergeant Vannes!"

"Here, sir!"

"Master Sergeant Hailer!"

"Here, sir!"

"Captain Evans!"

Silence.

"Captain Kermit Evans!"

A stifled sob from the front pew.

"Captain Kermit O. Evans!"

The moment hangs. Then, a call from the back of the church. *Fire in the hole!*

The Last Shot detonates danger-close. The explosive shock wave strikes the chapel, and the stained-glass windows of the sanctuary erupt and shatter inward. The blast rolls through the church, sunlight streaming in from above my head, and glass shards tinkle like diamond raindrops behind me. None of the brothers moves a muscle.

The December morning of the funeral at Arlington National Cemetery is bright, clear, and cold. My family liaison duties have started to wind down—the family was in Washington and had traveled there without me, Kermit is about to be buried, and there is little left to plan. I drive myself, attend the walk to the grave like anyone else. Arlington has an efficient system of several funerals a day. You are told where to park, where to gather, and when to move on. The crowd for Kermit is many times larger than I thought it would be—the Pentagon emptied of Air Force engineering officers, as it has been decades since one was lost in combat. The Army caisson carrying the casket, drawn by a team of horses, is followed by a parade of blue to the grave site, a brown and green grassy hill with regular dirt mounds, new looking and full of fresh headstones. This is not the shady, restful cemetery of a long-ago conflict. This is the bare, muddy, working cemetery of a country in the midst of war.

The funeral service is efficient and respectful. Flags are presented to Perneatha and Kermit's parents by the top two-star engineering officer in the Air Force. They play taps and fire a twenty-one-gun salute. The shots ring through your body, snap you awake to the realization that Kermit is about to be lowered into the ground. After the Arlington-organized portion of the funeral, the Masons come out and start over again. Kermit was a Mason, and special rites are now required. The service doubles in length, and the Arlington staff starts to get antsy. This wasn't in the schedule.

Then Perneatha's sister gets up to sing, as everyone walks by the casket. I don't remember any of the words, nor what song she sang. I would not be surprised if she does not remember either. I only remember the emotion, the grief and pure pain, the heartache, the loss. The family's hurt did not fit the Arlington schedule that day. It took many, many verses to just start to say good-bye.

My wife and I are walking through the airport in Colorado Springs. I'm working at Fort Carson, training another EOD unit for deployment. It's our fifth job at Fort Carson in three years: more men for the meat grinder.

My wife has been visiting me, taking a break from the kids, trying to reconnect with her Crazy husband. Our Marriage Counselor says we should do things together that we enjoy, start slow by just having fun. It's not my wife's fault that we struggle with this; I find little joy in anything.

Still, as we hold hands and walk together, it is clear that she is not looking forward to getting on the plane without me. I'm staring out into space, the Crazy feeling on a low boil, distracted, lost in my thoughts. My rifle hangs at my shoulder.

"What are you thinking about?" she asks.

"Kermit," I reply.

Her face betrays her shock. This is clearly not the answer she was expecting. We haven't talked about Kermit in a year or two.

"Why Kermit?" she asks.

How do I answer that I think about Kermit every day?

VII | *GUU-5/P*

THE THING IS, when you think you're Crazy, you don't always know that Crazy is the problem. Or that Crazy is what you should call it. At least not at first. Some guys are just angry all the time. Some get spooked and nervous. I thought I had had a heart attack.

What else do you think when you have pain in your left shoulder, and tightness in your chest, and feel like your heart is going to explode? The first time, when it starts with the pain on the left side, you wonder if you slept wrong or lifted too much weight at the gym. Then you realize just thinking about whether it's a heart attack makes it worse, your heart beating faster and faster the more you analyze. So you tell yourself that you're fine, not to be a hypochondriac, and move on with life.

But then it continues, the pain in the front left side and the back, and your wife gets nervous and tells you to go in to the emergency room at the VA hospital. So you do, and you get hooked up to the machines and have blood drawn, and after a couple of hours the doctor comes in to say you should just chill out and relax, like it's as easy as sitting in a chair and tuning out the kids and ignoring the foot in the box and reading a book and all your heart problems will go away.

Maybe the pain goes away for a while. Maybe other odd sensations come and go. A tightness in the neck. A pain in the jaw. A twitch of the eye. Always a twitch of the eye. Little symptoms, coming and going. How do you describe a gurgling that just feels wrong? Nothing specific—the aches and pains of getting old, you say, though your twenties are barely behind you.

Months pass, but then you have that day. Everyone has a day. My day was walking with my aunt through the Pearl District on the west side of Portland, Oregon. I stepped off the curb normal. When my right foot hit the pavement I was Crazy.

That odd combination of twinges, the unspecific aches, the random symptoms that sent you to the doctor over the years, suddenly combine in one overwhelming explosion. My chest flooded with emotional helium. It filled with an oppressive, overpowering distraction that pushed every rational thought from my head. Arm to arm, shoulder to shoulder, gut to neck, I blew up like a balloon. Not with pain, but with unnameable discomfort, a feeling—what feeling?—that demanded attention. I tried to ignore it. It sucked my brain of thoughts. I carried on with the day, but it intruded constantly. I slept, woke up, and it was there. It persisted, for a day, three days, a week. The feeling is intolerable. The persistence is intolerable.

A flight home, and on the plane I rocked and fidgeted as adrenaline bubbled and brewed. The more I thought about the feeling, the Crazy feeling, though I didn't know to call it that yet, the more it pervaded my every thought. My heart sped up, stopped, skipped, and pounded. I twitched and swelled all the way across the country. By that evening, I was back in the VA emergency room for a heart attack, throwing triple premature ventricular complexes on the beeping computerized heart monitor several times a minute.

But no heart attack had occurred. And the longer I lay in the emergency room, the younger and healthier I looked to the doctors and nurses, otherwise surrounded on that early Sunday morning by ailing drunks and lonely addicts.

"Go home and get some rest," they said.

"But what's wrong with me? Something is not right." On the monitor, my heart stopped for a moment to emphasize my point.

So the workups and testing and appointments began, stretching over the next month. An ECG that proved every vessel in my heart was opening and closing as it should. A stress test and take-home monitor that proved my heart was as fit as a teenager's. A blood test and fecal smear that declared I needed to get out in the sun more, but little else. Every test eliminated the worst physical possibilities. I had run out of doctor's appointments, and still the feeling persisted, three months on. Which left me one option.

It's all in your head.

But it was all in my chest.

Which meant I was Crazy.

Castleman was a reservist, a part-time EOD technician, and back home in Minnesota he was a full-time civilian firefighter. He said once a fire is waist high, you aren't going to extinguish it by hand. It just needs to burn itself out, or be sprayed with water by professionals from a fire truck.

We didn't have a fire truck. But we did have a shoulder-high fire, once we detonated the cache of old anti-aircraft rounds.

Twelve years of American aerial bombardment had taught Saddam to love anti-aircraft guns, ineffective though they were. He had them spread liberally throughout the country, in oil fields, cities, and open spaces. They decorated the countryside like lost and forgotten lawn ornaments, in various states of dry-rotting disrepair, random barrels sprouting from unlikely draws and pastures.

These anti-aircraft rounds were small, rusting, discarded. Left behind after the 57-millimeter gun itself had long been disassembled and sold for scrap. They were covered with dirt in a shallow hole in the middle of a farmer's field. The farmer knew they were there; he had plowed around them, probably for years. But now we had found them, and unfortunately could not ignore them. They were too dangerous to move and too dangerous to leave. It was quite unlikely they would be used in any IED, but you had to be sure. We had seen improvised grenades made out of 57s before—you just had to stick a simple fuze in the front end.

We knew there would be a fire before we blew them. There wasn't much helping it. The wind caught the flames right away and whipped the wheat field into a frenzy, blowing toward the primeval mud-walled village a couple of acres away. There was an irrigation ditch running in between, so it probably wouldn't spread. Probably. There was nothing we could do, so we left.

I never heard if our fire spread. Trey's certainly did. Two weeks later, when he blew a cordless-telephone/mortar combo on the side of a different road far west of Kirkuk, a spark snared the nearby wheat field, almost ripe with the winter crop. His fire didn't burn down the village, but it did destroy the entire harvest.

We didn't go to that village much before the fire, but we were back regularly afterward. The town rioted, and with no Americans available to slake their thirst for reprisal, the mob attacked the only symbol of governmental control available, storming their local Iraqi Police substation, killing everyone with a uniform inside. They hung the bodies in makeshift gibbets from the roof, and formed their own militia to guard the village from the attack they knew was coming.

The brigade did an air-assault mission with Shithooks and Black Hawks, prickly porcupines of rifles and machine guns and rocket launchers, to retake the village. We didn't destroy the village to save the village, but we came close. We eliminated the militia and moved new Iraqi Police back in. But there were IEDs on the roads leading to the town, with additional secondary hidden booby traps to kill the responding bomb technicians, for the rest of our tour.

"Maybe we should try not to burn down any more fields," I mentioned at dinner one night after the operation to re-seize the town.

"Maybe they shouldn't put out IEDs in the first place," was the unanimous reply.

When we invaded Afghanistan and Iraq, the Army and Marine Corps still fielded the M16A2, a gas-operated, air-cooled, magazine-fed, shoulder-fired rifle, as the primary weapon of many dismounts (soldiers operating on foot). The A2 was a variation on the Colt M16 famously first introduced in Vietnam. Although the internal mechanisms were updated, new NATO-compatible barrels installed, and open rear iron sights reconfigured with dials and compensators, it remained, to the uninitiated, basically the same weapon.

War, the true mother of invention, changed the rifle significantly. The M4, long in development and short on fielding, was widely introduced soon after the initial invasion. It was shorter and lighter, but still shot a single round or a three-round burst. Much to the delight of gear-loving soldiers, the M4 also had tons of external rails to bolt on extra equipment, such as optical sights, laser designators, and flashlights. The M16 was a long rifle, designed to kill targets several hundred meters away. The M4 was designed for urban combat, where size and weight are at a premium, and the enemy is much closer.

As an Air Force dismount, a term which would make no sense to those in charge, flying the planes, I carried the GUU-5/P, a Frankenstein of a weapon. The upper receiver, the top half of the weapon that carries the bolt assembly and contains the chamber, hailed from a first-production M16 from the early 1960s, slick with no forward assist and possessing a fully integral solid carrying handle on top. The lower receiver was hijacked from an M16A1, complete with fully auto trigger assembly. The collapsible stock came from a GAL-5 used by helicopter crews in Vietnam, and could cinch up quite small. The barrel was the newest portion, recently installed to comply with NATO regulations. We swapped out the hand grips on the barrel and bolted on after-market rail systems so we could mount laser sights, front pistol grips, and SureFires. Even after the modifications it was still shorter than an M4, but as loose as an old jalopy and in need of as much maintenance to keep it operational. Even the lowliest Fobbit—an Army soldier who never had a reason to leave the FOB—carried a shiny, never-used M4 to the chow hall every day, while we endlessly cleaned and resighted our antiques, twice the age of most of my brothers.

It was safe behind the wire, in the HAS, so we kept our rifles lined up on the gun rack right outside the door to the ops center. Grabbing your rifle meant it was time to go to work. It went on right after the body armor and stayed on, held tightly in place via slings and clips, pistol grip high. While outside the wire, conducting business, your right hand stayed nearly affixed to that grip, ready for use, all the time, until, with a sigh of relief, you shed the rifle at the HAS door upon return.

My rifle means it's time to do a job. It's time to focus, to observe, to stalk, to prepare, to react, to be ready for that constant song: incoming fire. If gunshots per IED call were a batting average, we'd win the Major League title every year. Potshots while driving through town ringing off the side of your truck. Zips and pings while crouched behind your Humvee, building an explosive charge with a cigarette hanging from your mouth and the robot ready to tear downrange. Single shots from a sniper in the center of Hawija. A sustained firefight while clearing a bridge. The soft breath of a stripper blowing on your neck, on the edge of your ear, a tingle across the very surface of your skin, then an answering shout from the .50-cal machine gun mounted on the security Humvee next to you. Gunfire in the distance. Gunfire in ambush. Gunfire to sing you to sleep.

The first time someone tried to kill me, I experienced a predictable flood of emotions. Fear. Anger. Worry for my brothers. I was not expecting to be confused. Why would they be trying to kill me, I thought. Don't they know it's *me*! That I have a wife and children? A mother who loves me and a house with a mortgage and a master's degree I haven't finished yet and plans to hike the Appalachian Trail someday with an old friend from Tennessee? If they only knew all that, they wouldn't try to kill me. They'd know it's me they were trying to kill, and they'd stop. They'd understand their mistake.

But they don't stop. They don't care, and soon you don't care, as confusion is swallowed by anger and purpose and an insatiable drive to complete the mission. And the robot clears the path under duress, and the car detonates, and the team downrange is extracted, and the town is seized and the EFP factory is turned over, and the more you are shot at the angrier and more determined you are. To go home. Everyone goes home. Fuck this place.

None of that changes one basic truth, however.

Every moment you are being shot at you are blissfully, consciously, wonderfully, tangibly alive in the most basic visceral way imaginable.

The pictures were grainy, taken with a cell-phone camera. Small, distorted, out of proportion a bit. The pillar and side-view mirror of the tan Suburban truck were also visible in a couple of them.

These guys actually drove down that street in a Suburban and took pictures of this place, I thought. Shit, they're crazier than us.

The pictures were grainy, but they were also unmistakable. Row upon row of EFP casings. Thousands of them. A line of straining baby-bird mouths, hungry maws reaching up and open, waiting to be packed with plastic Semtex. Waiting to be fitted with their copper-plate lenses. Waiting to be capped and riveted and strung up with det cord. Waiting to be encased in foam and hidden on the road. Waiting to be used on us.

Or waiting for us to come seize them first.

The raid was going to be big. Company sized, the largest operation our infantry brigade had undertaken in several months. A full perimeter of Humvees and armored trucks around fifteen square blocks in the southern industrial section of Kirkuk. A second infil with Shithooks and Black Hawks to seize several objectives. Buzzing Kiowas to monitor for anyone fleeing the scene and seeking to escape. And then us, and K9 dog handlers, and the spooks and special investigators to turn over each site once they were secure.

We didn't warn the Iraqi Army of the event, or ask for their assistance either; too easy for a mole to tip off the locals. For once, we wanted to surprise a known IED construction cell, actually catch someone before we bled. When the intel had come in I'd leaped out of my skin. The brigade was more sedate; they had been here longer, seen more, were more wary. For a week I begged them to do this op. I was sick of defense. Let's go on offense. The brigade eventually agreed. The opportunity for decisive success was too great to pass up.

"What do you think we'll find?" I asked Castleman as we loaded gear and grabbed our rifles, getting ready for the assault. I check my kit twice before every mission, but this was a big op, and we expected trouble. So I unloaded every rifle mag, checked the spring, and reloaded it with a mix of tracers and ball. I did the same with my pistol mags. I replaced my optical rifle-sight batteries, ensured that the rosary was in its pouch on my vest, and then checked everything from top to bottom a third time.

"We'll be lucky if those casings are still there by the time we arrive. They always seem to know we're coming," answered Castleman.

"There might be other stuff, though," I countered. "Lathes. Presses. Bang. Rivets. Forms to set the copper plates into the packed sleeves?"

"We'll see," said Castleman to no one in particular.

We arrived in the third wave to a scene of chaos, a swarm of dismounts and crowds of young men, half-dressed children splashing in muddy potholes, more oil than water, and helicopters making passes dizzyingly close to the ground. We pulled off the main highway into a tangled nest of car-repair joints, machine shops, and scrappers. The sun beat down relentlessly on the washed-out, crumbling concrete cells that passed for commercial storefronts. The narrow open bays faced each other across the dirty half-paved streets in a line, occasionally broken by alleyways that led to ramshackle sheet-metal slums. Your standard Third World paradise, in other words, dressed up with the occasional meager palm tree.

Our area to search was massive and time was limited by the mortar and rocket attacks soon to follow any U.S. action of this size. Our EOD team split up, I grabbed a spook to act as an extra shooter in case I got in a bind, and we made for the first automobile-repair place. On the way in we passed the previous occupants of the shops, a line of young men in polo shirts and loose pants, now sitting flex-cuffed and forgotten, left to bake in the midday sun.

It must be human nature to hoard when poor. Hovels in rat-infested slums the world over are humble on the outside but claustrophobia inducing on the inside, cramped and suffocated with all manner of junk and debris. Nuts and bolts and hand tools and jugs of grease and oil littered the floor. In one corner, a rickety frame and a chain system to hang engines. And then, behind a pile of discarded indiscernible automobile parts, a line of cylinder casings, neatly stacked and organized. But these were rusted, moldy, the wrong diameter, and too tall. They didn't match the evidence we had collected from previous post-attack investigations. These weren't right for the EFPs we had seen in the area at all. There must be another stash. Plus, no explosives. No lathes and presses. No top plates. No rivets. I moved on.

The next shop was the same. And the next. Endless heaps of tools and scrap metal. Open drains on the floor to collect piss and spent oil. The occasional pile of cylinder sleeves, but all ragged and worn out. My blood pressure jumped in one shop when I came upon a poster of New York City tacked to a wall. A cartoon tourist map you would find in a million tchotchke shops in southern Manhattan, several years old, as it still had the intact World Trade Center, noted as a tourist destination. But this wasn't intel, evidence of some new terrorist plot. It was decoration to brighten an otherwise hopelessly dank cellar.

I stepped outside into the brilliant sunshine and was momentarily blinded, so bright was the sun compared to the unlit work areas. I left to check in with others' results.

A terp dragged a flex-cuffed man through the alley from behind one of the engine bays and back into the center of the street. His head hung as the terp pulled him by the collar. I could see that both of his eyes were swollen shut, and he bled from his nose and mouth into the open gutter on the curb. From behind the shop, the sounds of additional interrogations echoed down the block, an object lesson to future subjects still bound and lined up in the sun outside on the street. I approached the terp.

"Did he say where the EFPs are hidden? Or where they are making them?" I asked.

"He says he knows nothing about EFPs," said the Kurdish terp in highly accented English. "But you must understand, sir, that he is an Arab, and therefore, a liar. You cannot believe anything he says."

I shook my head, and the terp noticed that I was about to leave. He reached out and grabbed my arm as I was turning away.

"But do not worry, sir," the Kurd said. "You can not believe him, but we will keep asking him questions anyway."

Castleman, Keener, and I leapfrogged from shop to shop,

across the street and back again, down alleyways and on roof-tops, exposed to a sniper's whim. The alarm clock in my head was ticking; we had spent too much time on-scene already. I dug through endless mounds of discarded scrap and poorly patched and mismatched power tools. In one shop we spot-ted a pile of slightly different casings—spun clean, shiny, new, and wrong. These weren't the casings we had seen on previous EFPs either. Nothing was right.

In the last shop on the block we found a stack of cylinder sleeves from floor to ceiling, marshaled six deep and twelve high. This was the cache from the grainy picture. The mother lode. What we had been sent to find.

And they were the same wrong cylinder sleeves we had found everywhere else.

I stepped outside and considered the scene again, hand on my rifle as gunfire awoke on the edge of town. The more shops we entered, the more the supposedly suspicious EFP casings looked like old rusting cylinder sleeves, waiting to be spun and milled clean to refit fresh piston assemblies, recycled parts for rebuilt engines. The more the nuts and bolts looked like nuts and bolts. The more the tools and dies looked like tools and dies. The more the machine shops looked like machine shops.

This wasn't an EFP factory.

"There's nothing here," I yelled over to Castleman in the next greasy stall.

"I agree," he responded. "I haven't seen a single scrap of bang or det cord or anything I'd call a trigger or an initiator. Just a bunch of rusty cylinder sleeves and a pile of shit."

"I found a mold for a drill press we can take." It was at the bottom of a pile of hand tools, with no drill press in sight. But it was flat on the top, non-mold end, and so could take a ham-mer as well.

"It's the only thing remotely suspicious," I said. "It's almost the right size. We'll see if they can randomly match it to anything at headquarters in Baghdad."

"What about all these sleeves we came for?" Castleman asked.

The rattle of incoming small arms echoed, still in the distance but moving steadily closer. I didn't want to stick around for the mortars.

"We're not blowing up four city blocks to get rid of a bunch of rusting engine parts from semi trucks, and we don't have the room to take them. They stay. This op was a waste."

Rounds were plinking off the Humvee by the time we had remounted and rounded up our escort security. We pulled away, leaving broken noses, swollen eyes, sore wrists, sunburns, and a smoldering resentment that seeped into the cracks and crannies of the surrounding neighborhood, a pall that hung like an ill fog.

When we arrived back at the FOB I went directly to the brigade ops center to provide a report on what we didn't find. There was little need; word had obviously already made it back. The Battle Captain met me in the hallway, red-faced and livid.

"I can't believe you *left* everything!" he practically screamed. "We had intel that those sleeves were being made into EFPs. We sent you there to seize them. What part didn't you understand?"

"What would you have had me do? Call for ten dump trucks and load them with every cylinder sleeve from every shop on the block? They have every right to fix engines in an engine shop! This is their livelihood!"

The Battle Captain was adamant.

"You have the blood of soldiers on your hands," he said, and the conversation was over.

I am at home, sitting on the landing on the second floor, staring down the narrow, quiet flight of stairs below me. My new son is sleeping in his crib in his blue room behind me. He is three days old. Tiny and pink and perfect. And helpless. Totally helpless. Someone could wring him like a rag and pull him limb from limb. Someone could pinch a little skin on his fat belly, twist and tear, and gut him like a shot duck. They could shake him until his head tore from his neck.

The Crazy stirs, and shows its spidery head.

That can't happen. I won't let it happen. No one will kill my son.

So I sit at the top of the stairs, with my rifle, and wait. I have picked a good spot. The narrow staircase has created a funnel, a choke point, where I can kill anyone coming up to the second floor.

My son is defenseless so I will defend him. I sit, and wait, and finger my rifle, and watch, all night.

The doctor wasn't helpful. He looked in the glass jar at the smashed scorpion, three inches long and translucent, and frowned.

"Well, it's either the kind that rots your skin off, or the kind that kills you," he said.

Twenty minutes earlier, turning off the water to the dribbling shower, I had thrown my towel around my shoulders to dry off. A shooting pain in my elbow. Another along my ribs. I jumped and shook and the scorpion fell out of a fold in the drab brown terry cloth. I smeared that scorpion on the wet plastic shower floor with my flip-flopped foot, grabbed the remains for evidence, and trotted back into the HAS still dripping wet. Pants and a shirt went on in a rush, and Griffin drove me to the FOB medical clinic moments later, the sting wounds growing a swollen red.

"Well, that sounds bad," I told the doc. "Can I get some meds?"

"Oh, we don't have the antivenom up here in Kirkuk," the doc replied with a wave of his hand. "And if we medevaced you on a bird now and it's the kind that kills you, you'll be dead before you got to Baghdad anyway. Do you know how hard it is to intubate in the back of a Black Hawk? Just go to your room and come back if you feel worse."

I told Griffin the verdict as we returned to the HAS. I wandered through the front blast doors, under the shady protective concrete canopy, in a daze.

"I'm going to go rack out," I told Griffin. "Please keep an eye on me. Just stop by every so often to see if I'm still breathing."

"Don't worry," Griffin said. "If you die in your sleep, we won't tell anyone. We'll take you out on a call and blow you up. You'll go out the right way."

I walk into my Old Counselor's office on the first floor of the Buffalo VA Hospital. But she's not my Old Counselor yet.

I've been in the VA a lot lately. Chest pain, blood draws, stress tests, EKGs, eye twitches, emergency-room runs for irregular heartbeats. Nothing for being Crazy. But I didn't know I was Crazy yet.

"Hi, I'm Brian. I'm checking in," I say to the middle-aged woman at the front counter.

"And what are you here for?" she asks.

"I have an appointment here but I don't know why," I answer. "It was made for me after my last ER visit a couple weeks ago."

"I see. Have a seat."

And I do. But the room doesn't feel right, and the Crazy feeling is gnawing at my heart.

My Old Counselor comes out to meet me, and beckons me into a closet-sized side room containing a foot in a box, two chairs, and a table. We sit.

"Do you know why you're here?" my Old Counselor asks. But she isn't my Old Counselor yet.

"I guess I've been using the ER too much?" I joke, and finger my rifle, and the Crazy jumps into my throat.

"Well, Brian, we just want to make sure everything is okay with you," my Old Counselor responds softly. "It can be really hard to transition back home, and everyone has their own challenges. I wanted to know if there was anything you wanted to talk about."

Gurgle. Swell. *Twitch*.

"Why would I need to talk about anything?"

I've figured out how I'm going to strap a pistol to the center console of our family's minivan. It can sit at my right knee, a modified old 9-millimeter drop holster bolted to the plastic next to the radio and cup holders. Discreet, out of the way, the grip angled up and ready for my right hand when needed. One thumb flick on a strap and it releases, heavy and comfortable and safe.

I need to get the pistol ready because I drive the minivan often, the kids to and from school every day, to the grocery store, the VA hospital. It is nearly impossible to shoot a rifle one-handed and drive at the same time. But with a pistol, I can either shoot out the lowered driver's window or, in an emergency, through the front windshield.

Reloading is tricky, as I drive with my left hand, but I have developed a work-around. In the back of my armored Humvee I kept a magazine pouch—six pistol mags and six rifle—strapped to the crossbar behind the driver's seat directly in front of me. Reaching forward to reload is already ingrained in my training. So if I find some heavy-duty Velcro tape I can put strips of the furry part on the very top of the dashboard, just to the right of the speedometer display. I'll then attach the bristly partner tape to the bottom of each pistol magazine. Then I can line up a couple of pistol mags, standing straight up, right in front of me and ready to go. When I need to reload, while still driving with my left hand, I can release the spent magazine with my right thumb, let it drop away into my lap, and slam the open grip of the pistol on the awaiting fresh magazine on the dashboard. With another thumb reach to the slider-release lever, the upper rail of the pistol slams forward, locks in the mag, round in the chamber, hammer back, and I'll be ready to fire again.

I've practiced a couple of times in my basement at home, and I can change magazines now without looking. The trick is to make sure the new magazine is fully seated in the pistol and clicks, so when you lift and pull it from its heavy Velcro latch, it doesn't fall out.

"You need to talk, Brian, because everyone needs to talk," my Old Counselor says.

She smiles weakly at me, her face lined and motherly, graying black hair and a soothing slump to her shoulders. The Crazy is boiling in my chest, and my hands shake, and I look down to see my foot bouncing on the floor.

"I have this feeling," I start. I don't tell her it's the Crazy feeling. Not yet. "It feels like my chest is swollen and my heart is going to burst. I don't know what it is. I don't know what causes it. But I can't stop it. And I can't control it. It's intolerable, and it's the only thing I can think about."

"Are you nervous? Or stressed?" my Old Counselor asks.

"No, that doesn't sound right. I'm not worried, and no deadline at work ever compares with combat."

"So why are you afraid?" she asks.

I laugh a stifled, uncomfortable laugh. My eye twitches. My heart gurgles.

"I don't spend a lot of time being afraid." Don't be scared of the soft sand. I chose this. I got to go back. I got everything I wanted. Don't be scared of the soft sand.

"What are you afraid of?" my Old Counselor presses.

I run up the hill, through the dust cloud, through the helicopter rotor wash, past the screaming women, through the piles of bodies discarded from countless car bombs, vest on, rifle in hand, ready, ready. But I can't run far enough away. I can't run fast enough to escape her question. Still I sit, in my Old Counselor's tiny office for the first time, the helium balloon in my rib cage about to explode.

"I'm scared of ending up like Ricky."

After that I tell her about Ricky. How we usually run together, and how he visits when he can. I go back the next week, and do the same thing all over again. And the week after that. And the week after that. Appointments pile on top of each other in a blur. Weeks become months, the winter becomes summer, the Crazy feeling endures, and still I cry in my Old Counselor's office until my grief and fear and detachment from the world has a name and a face.

Everyone poses with their rifles. Go online and search for it, or open any hardcover book on a recent conflict to the center section where they keep the photos, and you'll see. A line of young men, in vests and gear, helmets on or off, posing in front of a helicopter, or a statue of the disposed leader, or a blast wall, or a mountainside. The backgrounds vary. The faces are nearly identical; dirty smiles and short hair, average builds and day-old stubble. But one thing never changes. They always have their rifles. Hands on the grip, wrists bent, barrels down, cinched and tight on a sling or a retention strap.

You see the same pose struck in the background of photos of heads of state from the Third World. As the president-for-life moves from helicopter to armored car, or makes a speech in front of a blown-up building, they are there. Men with rifles, sunglasses, armored vests, short-sleeved shirts, khaki cargo pants, baseball caps. It's the uniform of the American merce-nary force of the twenty-first century, a group in which I now unexpectedly find myself. I conduct training, others still do the job. No matter. We call ourselves—active military and for-mer alike—by various names: operators, trigger-pullers, door-kickers, knuckle-draggers. All have the same rifle, in the same position, gloved hand on the grip, bent wrist, barrel down. All have the same look. The look of men who are willing to do things, have done things, are planning to do things, violent or extreme things that most do not contemplate. It is the willing-ness, the attitude, the consideration that matters. That is the important part.

Others have the look. I can see their rifles now too. Faded black-and-white plates from the days of Antarctic explora-tion. A line of men: dirty, sunburned, and frost-bitten faces; long beards and sunken eyes from months on the trail; a line of mushing sled dogs; a flag for their country; a sea of white behind them. And on each chest, a rifle hung, barrel down, stock to the shoulder. A photo mural of our local hockey team, writ large on the side of the arena downtown, a line of young men, jerseys half on, clad in armor and helmeted, each with a rifle, hands on the grips. On an Olympic podium, three competitors, three rifles.

It's in their eyes. They know. They feel the weight of the rifle as well.

Those were the three days that broke me. The three days that took my egg of innocence, precious and fragile, and crushed it under booted foot. On Monday we raided the EFP Factory That Wasn't. On Tuesday we survived the Day of Six VBIEDs. On Wednesday, Trey killed our first civilian, and I told him to do it.

The call came in like all the others. A truck bomb tried to ram a U.S. convoy in the giant traffic circle on the southern edge of Kirkuk, where the highways branch to Hawija to the west and Baghdad, ultimately, to the south. We had had the six car bombs the day before. To have only one truck bomb that day seemed easy. Trey took his team and, exhausted, I stayed in the ops center in the HAS, covered in coffee and reports.

But as the news trickled in it eventually became clear that the call was far from routine. A huge cordoned scene, the roundabout almost half a kilometer wide itself, and three highways' worth of traffic stopped and stewing. Multiple security teams—the U.S. convoy that got hit, special embedded units that the convoy was escorting, and Trey's security—only partially able to coordinate or communicate with each other. Small-arms fire that ranged from the usual sporadic to the periodically intense. And stuck in the middle, Trey, his EOD team, and a truck bomb that wasn't right from the start.

It was a white pickup, an innocuous small Toyota, no load

in the open bed, slumped on the side of the road where it had crashed after being riddled with bullets. The driver was also shot, draped against the dashboard, steering wheel pushing into his midsection. He just lay. And bled. And moaned. He wasn't dead. He might have been trapped. And he refused to even try to leave the truck, despite the gunfire. Despite the security. Despite the pleas and threats from U.S. terps over loudspeakers and bullhorns. He refused to talk or move or die.

Trey was a confident team leader, a southern good ole boy with a dip and a drawl and hound dog at home, a reservist who was a cop in civilian life, fearless and self-assured and independent; I rarely heard from Trey while he was on a call, and I rarely had reason to. There was little he couldn't handle. But this call was different. He checked back regularly to provide status updates. The tone of his voice changed, a slight quiver, an opening of ambiguity. He knew something wasn't right. Soon I was locked in the ops center and attached to the radio.

"This guy won't fucking get out," Trey crackled over the multiband radio.

"Can he get out?" I asked.

"I don't know, I'm sending in the robot now to check," Trey said.

A pause. A split second on scene, an eternity in the ops center, in the HAS, behind the blast walls and security cameras and armed guards.

"Captain, I can't tell if he's trapped, but there is another problem," Trey said. "I can't find the bomb."

"What do you mean?"

"I mean the bed is empty," Trey replied, "and I don't see anything through the robot camera in the cab either. There is no crush switch or suicide switch anywhere. So unless he stuffed it in the engine compartment that is crumpled in half, there is no bomb."

No bomb. We don't do traffic accidents, we do bombs. Still, you must be sure.

"So what do you want to do?" I asked Trey over the radio.

"The only way I can be sure there is no bomb in the cab is to explosively open it up. So he needs to get out of the truck, and I can't tell with the robot whether he even can. I need to go look. I'm going down," Trey said.

A solo approach to an IED, the tactic of last resort. We call it the Long Walk.

Trey's walk would be a run, in the open street and traffic circle, dodging the gunfire I heard continuously in the background. A run to the truck to pull a man out, a man that rammed a U.S. convoy an hour earlier and was shot for his trouble, to check for a bomb that might not exist.

Trey put the radio down. I gripped my mike tightly in my hand, and waited.

I was trapped in a plywood cage. I stared at the four walls, the map of Kirkuk tacked up on one, covered in red and blue pushpins. Three plywood desks, a whiteboard covered in notes, coffee cups and the remains of this morning's instant-oatmeal breakfast, papers with lists of equipment, call signs, and schedules. A rack of radios and amplifiers, a secure telephone, three "SECRET" computers and two "UNCLASS" ones. Price standing with his enormous arms crossed, a frown on his face. My rifle and pistol on the rack just outside the door.

None of it let me see what Trey saw. None of it saved Trey from taking the walk. None of it helped.

Price and I looked at each other in the ops center, and waited, because we could do nothing else.

I was never so grateful as when the radio speaker jumped back to life.

"Hey Captain, I was wrong. Number one, that mother-fucker's not trapped. Two, I saw a projo in the passenger foot well, stuck all the way up under there where the robot couldn't see it. He's got something there," Trey reported.

"Do you think it's a device?" I asked. Nothing small enough to be stuffed up behind the glove box could rightly be called a truck bomb. But something that small could easily have killed Trey if the driver had set it off while he was right there. But the driver didn't. Why?

"Could be," Trey said. "I don't know. I didn't see a trigger or wires or a battery at all. I just saw the artillery round. This guy could just be a mule, transporting it somewhere else. Or he could just be a scrapper."

Very few artillery rounds in Iraq had copper rotating bands anymore; they'd long since been clipped and plucked to sell for food money. Lately, we had seen a rise in people trying to sell the steel casing of the rounds themselves, some with the explosives still inside. We ran off kids from our demolitions area regularly, drawn not by curiosity but by direction from their family to retrieve the scrap iron we had, before or after we completed our disposal detonation. There is nothing worse than watching children run toward your pile of projos and mortars, covered in explosives set to blow and with the fuze cooking.

"He could be a scrapper, but we can't take that chance," I said.

"He's still not leaving the truck, though, and the small-arms fire around here is getting worse," Trey said. "What should we do?"

"I'll tell you what we're going to do. We're going to Boot Bang it."

Taking apart bombs is our business. Killing people is usually security's business, but it was about to be ours. Mine. I needed to take responsibility for the decision, put it on my shoulders, for whatever would happen after.

I made a phone call to the Battle Captain at the Battalion TOC, who managed the war second by second.

"Hey, you know what's happening at the traffic circle?" I asked.

"Sure do. Why haven't you safed the IED yet?" he asked.

With the Army, it always seemed so simple. We made every IED problem go away, it was just a matter of time. Usually too much time for them.

"Yeah, we've got a problem. The driver won't leave the truck. If we set off our explosive tool under the truck with him in it, it's going to kill him."

"So what's the problem?" the Battle Captain asked.

"The problem is we take apart bombs, we don't use them, and our tools aren't for killing people. I need to be sure everyone is comfortable with us making an exception this time. That you know this guy is going to die when we blow the truck."

The Battle Captain seemed confused.

"We already tried to kill him, and shot him at least once," the Battle Captain said. "He's going to bleed out anyway, probably. If he wants to sit on the bomb when you clear it, that's his choice. Are you asking for approval? Yeah, sure. Whatever. Go ahead. Do whatever you need to do."

The Battle Captain hung up.

Whatever we needed to do. I imagined how many pieces that driver would be in after we lit up this shot. Boot Bangers weren't designed for trucks, but that little Toyota didn't stand a chance against one. Whatever was inside would soon be out. Which included the driver, in pieces, most likely. If the charge was directly under him it would likely vaporize his lower half and send the upper chunk up through the roof, out of the truck just like the bomb components we sought to disrupt. But since the artillery round was under the passenger side, Trey would likely put the charge a few more feet over. The driver would then probably stay in one large piece, peeled back and inside out like a dressed deer that has been hung by the leg from a tree and skinned. But his body would be easier to recover, smashed into the ceiling and driver's door but mostly intact. If we were really lucky, his lungs would simply explode from the tremendous blast over-pressure, and his body would barely have a scratch. Not likely at this range.

I called Trey on the radio.

"You have the green light. Put the Boot Banger under the cab."

The wait again was agonizing, as Trey's team built the charge and the robot dragged it down to the truck.

"Captain, the Boot Banger is down there," Trey said. "The robot is working on sliding it under the passenger side now."

"When it's under, don't wait," I said. "If the shot placement is good and where you want it, you have permission to crank it off whether he's in the truck or not."

"Hold on, Captain, something's happening," Trey said, his voice trailing away at the end.

One of Trey's team members left the open mike on.

"Wait, he's getting out now! Where's the terp? Tell him to move away from the truck. Good. Now tell him to stop. I said, tell him to stop. He needs to fucking stop. Tell him he needs to stop coming towards us. He can't approach us. I will shoot him if he approaches. Tell him that. He's got something under his man-dress. What's he doing? Fuck!"

Two shots. Two shots only.

Trey shot him at a hundred meters, one in his chest, one in his head. It was a Koran under his man-dress, we discovered later. Trey only finished what several of us started. The driver wasn't going to live through that day, and he probably knew it.

Sick of being a stationary target for the constant rain of incoming bullets, Trey simply burned down the pickup truck and left. It didn't detonate, so it probably wasn't a bomb, but we never found out.

Objective is white two-story house, fifty meters, directly ahead. Dismount. On me, to the door! Stack up! Stack up! Front door barred. Breacher to the door! Fire in the hole in three . . . two . . . one . . . *Boom!* Go! Go! Go! Go! Clear left! Stairway up. Watch where you're sweeping! Covering left. Clear right! You, doorway. You, stairway. You and EOD, with me. Up the stairs. Go! Go! Go!

Get the fuck down! Put the fucking gun down! Get the fuck down! Tell this bitch to shut up! *Kef! Kef!* Where's the terp? Get the terp up here! Tell that kid not to move. Tell him to stop right now or I'm going to shoot him. Tell him, and get that bitch to shut up.

Where are the explosives? Ask him where he's keeping the IEDs and explosives. The things that go boom. Don't fucking lie to me! Tell him not to lie to me. We know they're here.

How can you let your kid play with a gun, like a toy? What the fuck is wrong with you people? Don't you realize I almost shot him? I almost shot your fucking kid. Goddamn. Did you tell him that? This fucking place.

You found it? In the dirt floor, on the ground level? Good. We're blowing up this fucking house. They won't hide shit anymore. Where's the terp? Tell them to get out of the house. That we're blowing up his fucking house, and he's going to jail. The wife and kid can leave, I don't care. Let them go, but take that kid's gun first.

You ready to go? Big explosion? Cool. Let's get down.

Fire in the hole! Fire in the hole! Fire in the—*Boom*—hole! Fuck it, let's get out of here.

I simply exist from moment to moment. There is no meaning in my past. My present is intolerable. I don't expect my future to exist.

I simply run, with Ricky, every day, to cloud with pain what would be immediately exposed without constant distraction.

When the depravity of this world is laid before you in its ruin, and you discover yourself mired in it, rather than above, what hope do you have? All that my feeble actions until now have produced is misery for myself, my children, my wife, and the children of thousands I do not know.

I'm on the road again, conducting training in another faceless city, sitting in a blank hotel room. My wife pleads with me on the phone.

"Please," my wife begs, sobbing between words. "Please, just cheat on me while you're gone. Please, just go do it. Let me leave you with a clear conscience. Free me and the children. I can't follow you into this dark place."

I put down the phone without answering. I'm too scared to cheat and leave, and so we endure.

The Buddhists say that you must let go of all things. That you must remove your attachment to worldly possessions, and to your professional successes, and even to your loved ones, before you can be free of pain and suffering.

I am utterly detached from the world. I am invested in nothing. I should be steps from enlightenment.

But I am only Crazy.

VIII | *The Science and the Chakras*

THE MEDICAL DOCTORS and researchers first noticed the phenomenon in Serbia and Bosnia, following the war in the early 1990s, the first conflict in which modern western armies with modern armor and equipment met modern western medicine. Soldiers on both sides survived explosive detonations that would have killed in World War II, Korea, or Vietnam. Body armor and helmets caught frag, armored vehicles survived blasts, and soldiers walked away seemingly unhurt from what would have been death sentences two decades before.

But they were not unhurt. The symptoms of their injuries only appeared later. Doctors in Serbia noticed odd combinations of complaints from veterans of the Balkan War in the old Yugoslavia. Headaches that wouldn't go away. Lost memories, or challenges forming new ones. Personality changes. The inability to make a decision or solve problems. Sleeping disorders, insomnia, or nightmares. Some had mild complaints that merely hindered daily life. Some could barely function at all.

The soldiers had a new kind of wound, a kind not previously recognized because no victim that had ever received one survived long enough to tell about it. The name for this new condition? Blast-induced Traumatic Brain Injury.

TBI had previously been known to aging football players, boxers, or victims of car accidents and falls from high places. In each of those cases a concussion occurred, a condition familiar to doctors and lay people alike. During a concussion the brain slams into the interior of the skull, either because a hard object struck the skull directly, or because the skull was moving very quickly and then came to a sudden stop. The initial symptoms of concussions are well known: headaches, vomiting, disorientation. The long-term effect, concussion-induced TBI, is less understood, but sustaining multiple damaging incidents increases the risk for permanent debilitating brain damage and Parkinson's-like effects.

But the skull and brain are built to survive injuries of this type. There is an evolutionary need for our tree-dwelling ancestors to still find food after an accidental fall to the ground on their heads. Concussions are natural events that our body is prepared for. Blast waves from a detonation, on the other hand, are not naturally occurring. We have no intrinsic defenses.

A blast wave is a glorified sound wave, and obeys all the same basic laws of physics. It can bounce and reflect. It dissipates rapidly over distance. And it can travel through objects, like the human body. When a blast wave vibrates through a substance—walls, cars, human tissue—it moves at a speed related to the density of the material through which it is traveling. Air is not dense, and so the blast wave moves relatively slowly, though still several thousand feet per second, depending on the type of explosive used to produce the blast wave initially. Concrete walls and fluid-filled organs are dense, however, and the blast wave speeds up in these materials. The damage to the material, and thus the body, comes at the barrier between dense and airy substances.

Imagine you are standing too near a car bomb detonating

on a city street. When the blast wave enters your gut, it speeds up through the outer skin of the human body, through the fluid-packed muscle of the abdominal wall, and into the colon. But there it finds open air, and slows down, causing shearing, ripping, and tearing. The same trauma occurs when the wave reenters the opposing colon wall, and so on throughout the body. At each density junction, shear forces and rapid expansion and contraction cause devastating injuries. Small and large intestines hemorrhage and bleed internally. Kidneys disconnect from fragile connecting tissue and fail. Delicate alveoli rupture and fill the lungs with blood, suffocating the victim. And in the brain, even small blast waves can have large consequences.

Scientists and doctors once considered the brain a big fluid-filled organ, no different in this respect than your liver, and relatively resistant to blast damage. Then Bosnia happened, and injured veterans presented never-before-seen symptoms of brain trauma. When a blast wave enters the head, it speeds up at each threshold, through the skin and the skull and the bag of cushioning fluid that surrounds the two main lobes of the brain. Then the wave encounters tiny nerve endings, neurological fibers, and slight synapses. Faced with a couple of billion density junctions, it shears, strains, rips, and tears its way to the back of the skull and out the other side.

The soldier who experiences this trauma is often unaware of it. If he is caught close to a large detonation then fragmentation damage to the rest of his body is the first concern—he may be bleeding from amputated stumps or body puncture wounds. If he is in an armored truck, he may be thrown about inside the steel box, slamming his helmeted head into the ceiling and suffering a standard concussion in addition to any blast-induced damage. In both cases, it is only after the immediate acute injuries are treated and survived that the long-term TBI nightmare becomes apparent.

The most insidious damage, however, occurs during missions where you think you're fine. Where you see the pavement erupt in front of your vehicle as you scream down a lonely Iraqi highway. The driver notes the danger too late, tries to stop and swerve, but the windshield suddenly fills with smoke and debris as the blast wave overwhelms the front of the truck. Your chest thumps, your ears ring, and your head splits under the weight of the *crack*. Chunks of asphalt embed themselves in the armored glass, and pieces of bumper and grille and headlight are torn and scattered. Your front tire thuds into and out of the newly created crater as your vehicle finally grinds to a halt. You pat yourself down; all fingers and toes accounted for. No blood or missing pieces. Your harness kept you locked to your seat. The radio jumps to life. Are you all right, the convoy commander wants to know. Is everyone fine?

You look at the driver, he looks at you. You both laugh, as the adrenaline takes over and you start to shake. Fuck yeah, you're fine. Luckiest sons of bitches on the planet.

But you are not fine. Inside your head, nerve connections that used to exist have been torn and broken. If the blast was close and more damage done, you may have lost parts of high school geometry, the coordination needed to tie flies for your fishing reel, or the ability to make decisions at the supermarket about what meat to buy. If you are lucky, you only lost your son's first steps or the night you asked your wife to marry you.

And if you are a bomb technician, one of my brothers, chances are you don't have only one lucky scrape, only one detonation where you were a little too close. You have dozens. Or hundreds. Spray-foam-encased EFPs that detonate while you are trying to disrupt them. Daisy-chained 130-millimeter artillery rounds that hit your vehicle on the way to a call. Truck bombs you choose to detonate, but must be unnervingly close to, watching and guarding and keeping children from drawing too near in a dense city center. Large-scale demolition to destroy hundreds of tons of stockpiled arms found in caches. Detonations in training when you are preparing to deploy in the first place. Every day, something is blowing up. Every day, your brain rips just a little bit more.

Blast waves tear up memories and functions. They leave holes where your identity used to be. You lose parts of your past and have trouble retaining the present or remaking a future. The strong, capable soldier now can't sleep, can't discern or differentiate among voices and noises, becomes easily distracted, gets tired, cries randomly in public, and doesn't know what to order for dinner. Where does Crazy stop and TBI begin? Who knows?

The good news is that your brain can regrow paths and you can reclaim skills you've lost. Particularly bad TBI victims, those who have lost the ability to speak or walk, often eventually relearn those skills after months and years of grueling therapy. But the new pathways are longer, more complex, and take more energy to use. Those with blast-induced TBI can experience fatigue of many varieties and intensities. This fatigue isn't like being tired after a long workout. This fatigue is being so tired you can't get out of bed, into the shower, can't make breakfast or summon the energy to dial a phone. Some have difficulty completing the most basic tasks of daily living. Some just have trouble concentrating, doing a complicated task for long periods of time. Your brain literally hurts because it is tired. It has had to work much harder, fire neurons over a much greater distance than before the injury. You no longer have some of the efficient neural pathways laid down in infancy, as you taught yourself how to lift a red block and set it on a blue one. Now your brain runs a marathon to do the same task. If you are lucky like me, then the fatigue and pain just set in after a long day of thinking, of solving complex problems or learning new skills. Your mind and body are exhausted from the process. It hurts in a way that overwhelms my ability to communicate.

I'm not just Crazy. I have a broken brain exhausted from fixing itself.

My New Shrink and I are doing a guided-meditation session. I haven't relaxed in months, and this is supposed to help. I sit in my upright chair, close my eyes, and try to concentrate on her words.

"First, feel your left thumb," she says. "Flex your left thumb. Make it as tight as you can. Good. Now relax it. Now your left index finger. Slowly now. Feel the tension build in each finger, and your whole hand, and then release it.

"Release the tension and relax," she says.

But I can't relax. I've already flexed my left arm and right thumb and right hand and right arm and gut and legs and feet before she has made it above my elbow. And anyway, I can't flex the Crazy, and I can't release it.

"Good," my New Shrink says, assuming I have followed along with each individual step instead of skipping ahead to the end.

"Now we breathe," she says. "Breathe deeply into the base of your stomach. Breathe into your entire rib cage. Breathe into the base of your spine. And relax."

But I don't relax. The Crazy expands in my chest. I breathe

deeply and it fills with Crazy. I exhale completely, but my rib cage is still full.

"Open your collarbones. Be present. In your mind," she says.

My mind is aware. It sits behind my closed eyelids, staring into nothingness. It directs the tension, the breath. It sees through the darkness.

But my mind is not centered. It is not balanced, does not lie equally behind my eyelids. It drifts, first barely favoring the left eye over the right, then slipping further to the side, then abandoning the right completely. My mind sits to the left of my eyes, looks back at an angle at the black void stretching endlessly before my physical body's line of sight. I sit beside myself and breathe.

My New Shrink tells me to open my eyes.

"How was that?" she asks. "Do you feel more relaxed?"

I describe how my mind drifted away from behind my closed eyelids. How I stared into the depths off-balance.

"Fascinating!" she exclaims.

It is the birthday of my fourth son. He is two today, and the family has come over for a party. Grandma and Grandpa, aunt and cousin. Even Ricky unexpectedly stopped over, the first time he was able to come. His little daughter is four now, growing up too fast, though she couldn't make the party.

The two-year-old is gleefully unwrapping presents, discovering puzzles and games and cars. He opens a red stuffed animal, and with a squeal, dives on top of it and rolls around on the carpet, his older brothers tickling and giggling with him.

I don't remember any of their second birthday parties.

I concentrate on the sights and the sounds and I check my

rifle. I gulp it in, watching, analyzing, encoding. Burn this one in, Brian. Remember it.

My wife is pulling out the camera and elicits a "cheese" from the tangle of arms and legs on the floor. Grandpa is in search of another piece of cake. Grandma watches with a small smile on her lips.

But it's already starting to slip away. A fading echo. I concentrate harder.

Remember it, Brian!

I grasp the slipping sand with both hands. There are plenty of gaps for this party to fill, but my bucket has a hole in the bottom, and by the end of the day, it's nearly gone.

I died in Iraq. The old me left for Iraq and never came home. The man my wife married never came home. The father of my oldest three children never came home. If I didn't die, I don't know what else to call it.

I liked the old me, the one who played guitar, and laughed at dumb movies, and loved to read for days on end. That me died from a thousand blasts. Died covered in children's blood. Died staring down my rifle barrel, a helpless woman in the crosshairs and my finger on the trigger. That me is gone.

The new me is frantic and can't sit still. The new me didn't laugh for a year. The new me cries while reading bedtime stories to my children. The new me plans to die tomorrow. The new me runs almost every day, runs till knees buckle and fail. The new me takes his rifle everywhere. The new me is on fast-forward. The new me is Crazy.

The new me has a blown-up Swiss-cheese brain, and doesn't remember all of the old me. But he remembers enough.

Enough to be ashamed. Enough to miss the old me. Enough to resent the old me. Resent the way everyone mourns him, while I am standing right in front of them.

Do you remember when Daddy used to? That daddy is gone. He doesn't do those things anymore. Do you remember when we used to be happy? Husband isn't happy anymore.

Maybe my wife should pull out the letter I left for my sons and read it to them. Maybe it would explain why Daddy didn't come home.

When you go to war, and die, and come home Crazy and with a ragged brain, you get to watch your family carry on without you.

Everyone longs for the old me. No one particularly wants to be with the new me. Especially me.

The yoga studio is on the second floor of a rather dingy 1960s-era retail box. This flat storefront, uniform block and picture windows, sits dissonantly in a neighborhood of historic wrought iron and brick, the wide squares and monuments of downtown Savannah, my two-week home while on the road teaching at the local Army post. Thin worn carpet covers the creaking stairs leading up to the stifling studio. It's summer in the South, and the heater is on. Intentionally.

My New Shrink first suggested the yoga. It holds the symmetry and release I crave. The muscle strain boils off the Crazy. The repetition dulls, then frees, the mind. On a bad day, the forms demand all of my concentration: my legs shake, my arms twitch instead of my eyes, and I hold the Crazy at bay for another hour. On a good day, the flow reverses the Crazy for a moment and my healing mind is present beneath and apart from the movement. Yoga is club and scalpel. Yoga is exhaustion and insight.

My Yogini likes hot yoga, and she has the space heaters cranking in the wide hardwood-floored space. I strip as far as public modesty allows, and the sweat builds on my brow even as we sit, cross-legged, waiting to begin our practice.

The Yogini walks to the front of the room and sits on her own mat, crossing her legs and placing her feet on the top of her thighs. She is younger and shorter than I, athletic, confident, with a high calm voice and the gift of putting everyone around her at ease. I would find her presence and choice of tight clothing distracting if I weren't so embarrassed at being Crazy.

"We start our yoga practice by breathing the word 'Om,'" my Yogini begins. "When you say your Om, pull it from the deepest part of you. Press your hips and flesh into the earth below us. Your Om comes from there, up through your body, through your lungs and out of your mouth."

I sit flat and wide and prepare my Om as best as I know how.

"We will send our Om into the universe," says the Yogini. "Our Om will join and harmonize with all that is. Then we will let it go."

She takes a deep breath, and an enormous Om, astonishingly loud and deep, erupts from the small form seated in front of me. The rest of the class joins, choosing her octave or another above or below.

My breath fills my lungs all the way down into my stomach, and I self-consciously release my Om. My voice is deep, but my Om does not resonate. It is thin and tempered.

"Do not judge your Om," the Yogini says in my mind, but the Crazy does not let go easily.

When our collective Om is a memory of an echo, and hot humid silence has returned, the Yogini begins the *vinyasa,* the flow, the sequences of poses and forms that exhaust and renew mind and body.

Tadasana. Uttanasana. Chaturanga Dandasana. Urdhva Mukha Svanasana. Adho Mukha Svanasana. Tadasana.

Mountain. Standing Forward Bend. Plank and lower. Upward Dog. Downward Dog. Feet forward. Mountain. Repeat your *vinyasa.*

Tadasana. Uttanasana. Chaturanga Dandasana. Urdhva Mukha Svanasana. Adho Mukha Svanasana. Tadasana.

I have to think about the forms at first, watch my hand placement, concentrate on the turn of my arm, stretching my legs, pulling the *Ujjayi,* the Sounding Breath, from deep in my belly. The first *vinyasa* is clumsy; my muscles' thoughts are full of rifles and pistols and transitions between the two, and my body struggles to remember the forms. On the second *vinyasa* the sweat is already building, oppressive heat turning skin sheen to stream. The third aligns my breath and movement. The fourth I don't remember.

I spend more and more of my time at the VA hospital now. Tall, gray, in four wings with a skullcap cupola at the top, Buffalo's veterans hospital is a monolith to sorrow and loss; that mausoleum could double in size and it still wouldn't be big enough to contain the misery it houses. I started as a patient in the emergency room for heart trouble. But it turns out it was Crazy, not Cardiac. So now I go to Mental Health on the tenth floor instead of Internal Medicine on the eighth.

The longer elevator ride gives you momentary relief to feel healthier, comparing yourself with other patients. Decrepit

World War II veterans, amputees from combat or diabetes, slumped in their wheelchairs and dressed in flimsy gowns and baseball hats denoting their last ship or unit. Vietnam veterans, always in insulated camouflage jackets keeping out the winter chill, covered in patches that read "These Colors Don't Run" and "Never Forget" to honor POWs and MIAs. Younger guys, dark jeans and too-short hair, taking the trip all the way to Ten with me. One guy has a tan T-shirt with a comic-book-style drawing of a soldier, full kit, hand on his rifle, his amputated right leg replaced with an ergonomic flexible running prosthetic. Alongside is written "You should have killed me when you had the chance."

You look at the floor. So do they. You check your rifle. So do they. You walk up to the same check-in counter. You sit in the same waiting room. You wait your turn to talk about your Crazy. In silence.

Today I turn away from the Behavior Health office and head to Neuro-Psych testing. It's the next step in my evaluation. How much of me being Crazy is a shredded brain?

I enter the smallish office and sit across from a young, dark-haired PhD. She writes down my medical history, deployment history, occupation, and stressors, using a long, just-sharpened pencil on a crisp white form. We're probably the same age, but today, sitting in that chair and after the elevator ride, Crazy following in my shadow, I feel twice as old as the fresh-faced promising girl across the table from me.

"What did you do in the military?" the PhD asks.

"I took apart bombs." It's my standard reply now.

"How often?"

"Most days. Some days were worse than others."

"And you were safe while you did this," she assumes innocently.

I'm not sure how to answer that.

"Well, the enemy is trying to kill you. So no, not really." It's the best I can do.

She looks confused.

"So you didn't decommission bombs? These are bombs the enemy made?" she asks.

I think she is starting to get it.

"Right. Those roadside IEDs you hear about on the news."

"So every day you thought you were going to die?"

"You could say that."

Furious note scribbling.

"So when was your traumatic brain injury?" she asks.

"All the time."

"What do you mean?"

"I blew up something every day. Sometimes the enemy tried to blow us up. Sometimes we were far enough away. Sometimes we weren't."

More furious note scribbling.

"I bet OCD is useful in your job," she notes.

"Yeah, it can be." Less useful now.

"We don't get a brain like yours in here very often," she concludes.

Is that a good thing, I wonder.

We get up and she leads me to the testing station. An empty desk, white walls, a pale institutional notepad, four yellow number-two pencils. For three hours I repeat numbers in order, memorize obscure lists of animals and vegetables, do mental arithmetic, draw geometric figures, and then recall those animal and vegetable names again. Zebra giraffe cow squirrel onion celery cabbage spinach. See, I can do it now.

Why can I remember shapes and vegetable names, but not the events of my life as I live them?

The problem isn't that I'm dumb. The problem is that I'm Crazy. This doesn't seem to be a test for that.

Now we move to a nearby large, boxy desktop computer station where she calls up an antiquated blue-and-white text program. I'm supposed to rate my feelings of worry and stress. Now we're getting somewhere.

Do your hands shake? Do you feel on edge? Do you have trouble sitting still? Do you fear people are out to get you? Do you feel scared to go outside? Terrified of the future? Do you have trouble sleeping? Do you relive traumatizing experiences while you are awake?

No questions about eye twitches. No questions about gurgles. No questions about carrying your rifle everywhere you go.

Certainly no questions about the Crazy feeling.

I finish the computer screening unsatisfied and go to the glaring fluorescent basement cafeteria for an early lunch of overcooked chicken, waiting for my test results and screening scores to come back. I hope for a positive result, a positive find, a massive failure of some orb or cortex. I pine for a physical reason for the Crazy symptoms. Physical damage to my head would finally be an explanation, a reason, a scapegoat. I finish my limp broccoli and return to the doctor's spare office on the tenth floor.

My results are spread out before the pretty PhD. The check marks are mostly on the right-hand side of the handwritten white page. I maxed out the test one way or the other.

"Every brain is built differently, and every brain is damaged differently," the PhD says. "Most people would be thrilled to have your spatial and cognitive abilities. We don't know how your brain worked before, but we know it works fine now."

"So, I don't have a TBI?"

She considers.

"No, you probably have some damage. No one could do what you did and not have damage. It's just not impairing your short-term memory or reasoning," she says.

Giraffe Zebra Cow Squirrel Spinach Celery Onion Cabbage. No, I guess not.

"What about the long-term memory?"

"I'm not in your head," she says. "I don't know what used to be there. I don't know what you lost, and there is no way to test for it."

"But there is something wrong. What is it?"

"The problem isn't your brain," she says. "The problem is how you react to your brain."

So I'm Crazy. But I knew that already.

The sweat is pouring down my face now in a stream, stinging my eyes, hanging and dripping off my nose, my mat slick in front of me.

Tadasana. Uttanasana. Chaturanga Dandasana. Urdhva Mukha Svanasana. Adho Mukha Svanasana. Tadasana.

Tadasana. Uttanasana. Chaturanga Dandasana. Urdhva Mukha Svanasana. Adho Mukha Svanasana. Tadasana.

I lose count of *vinyasas.* The flow loosens my binds, frees my mind from the cage of the now-distracted body. It moves with my *Ujjayi,* the Crazy forming a puddle on the floor.

My mind follows my Om, of breath and flecked with spit, released into the universe, back through time, no time, the continuum of the river flowing, no start or end. My mind flows upstream, dips into the HAS at Kirkuk, to a call coming, to the rhythm of timeless combat.

The Warrior is called and the Warrior goes. It has ever been so. Who will go? I will go.

When the call comes in, the ballet begins. First, the armor. My *dō*, my cuirass, my armored vest first. Then shoulders, *sode,* strapped and down. *Tekko* on my hands. My *kabuto* on my head. Thousands of times before. Thousands of times again. A miasma of ages but the same dance. *Katana* and *wakizashi,* broadsword and dirk, rifle and pistol. It has been ever thus, in our human river flow. My Om is their Om.

Rifle in hand, *suneate* on my shins, *Chaturanga Dandasana.* My *vinyasa* flows out of the HAS, to meet security, to go on the call, to meet the challenge. Girded with breastplate and mail, the shake and clank of metal on metal, we meet in a circle, surrounding the Chaplain, the Padre, the sanctifier of our mission, on one knee, head down, rifle inverted to forehead. A cross over our helmets, a blessing before battle. *In Nomine Patris, et Filii, et Spiritus Sancti.* Rifle stock, barrel, magazine, optics. The flow continues.

Tadasana. Uttanasana. Chaturanga Dandasana. Urdhva Mukha Svanasana. Adho Mukha Svanasana. Tadasana.

My grandfather runs from the landing craft onto the cold, storm-racked beach. His plane lands on the jungled island, a speck upon the wide peaceful sea. He charges up the mosquito-infested Virginian killing field. He falls in the black forest.

I am but a drop in the river. My Crazy is but a drop in a drop in the river. My Crazy has always been, if not in me, then in the river. The flow continues.

Tadasana. Uttanasana. Chaturanga Dandasana. Urdhva Mukha Svanasana. Adho Mukha Svanasana. Tadasana.

Blessed and mailed and armed and mounted, we charge to the call.

When we got to the deserted street corner in southern Kirkuk the Iraqi Police were already on scene, shooting at the IED with their AK-47s.

"How many times have we told them they can't do this anymore?" I vented in frustration, to no one in particular.

"It's their country and they'll do what they want," Castleman replied. "But if they don't quit it now we're leaving."

The Iraqis lacked robots and training, and so shooting at an IED with a rifle was an attractive option to the desperate or slightly sane. The more typical Iraqi Army soldier or policeman, however, had little compulsion with invoking *Insha'Allah* and simply walking up to the IED and cutting it apart by hand. This is precisely what happened, in fact, as Mengershausen unloaded the robot and I started to build an explosive charge. Castleman was still chatting over security requirements with our local infantry fire team when a plainclothes cop walked up to us with a plastic box in his hand.

"It is okay now," he said in broken English. "It is safe now. All done. I do it. Okay now. You go home."

"What's okay now?" I asked, taking the plastic box from the Iraqi policeman.

"I cut it off the bomb. No boom. It's all okay," he replied.

"Where is the bomb you cut it off of?" I asked, a bit more directly.

"Right there, you see it," he said, and pointed to a large concrete block sitting in front of a pile of garbage not twenty yards away. Too close, too close.

I resisted the urge to throw the potentially dangerous bomb component away like a live grenade and instead looked at it closely. A black plastic box the size of my fist, large enough to hide triggering components. Several heavy-gauge white and red wires, the ends recently sheared from this cop's knife, led from holes in the box. But something didn't look right.

"Where was this box?" I asked again.

"On the side. On the bomb. Right there. I cut it off. It's all okay now. Very good for you now," the young cop insisted.

I recognized this particular policeman. He was one of their nominal detectives and leaders, with a slight build and embarrassingly thin moustache on his sweating upper lip. I didn't trust any Iraqi policeman, and they didn't trust us, but this one was a Kurd, and he had never specifically led us into any trouble that I knew of. Younger than me, but he probably had a brood of eight kids and a wife at home in some hovel across the river. They all did.

I looked at the box and I looked at the IED he had indicated. Why would the bomber put an easily accessible trigger mechanism on the outside of otherwise solidly encased concrete? The heavy block itself was now flecked with divots and cracks, evidence that the police had been shooting at the device for a long time but had made little headway at breaking it apart. Why would the bomber give us an easy target to remove?

I looked up at the rest of my team. Mengershausen had the robot nearly on top of the concrete block now, and was reaching toward it with one heavy stainless-steel arm. Explosive workups done, Keener was mounted in his normal spot behind the steering wheel. Castleman was out in the open, looking at the concrete block through binoculars, guiding Mengershausen in. To our north, west, and south dense, impenetrable slums and faceless tenements closed us in. To our east lay the river, and beyond, on the far bank, onlookers gathered on rooftops of shanties, watching our every movement. Watching and waiting.

"Hey, Castleman, check this out," I called, and threw him the black plastic box.

Castleman caught it, looked it over once, and then popped it open with a flick of his knife tip. The plastic box was empty. The wires led inside to nothing; they were simply knotted and tied off, so they wouldn't fall out.

It was a hoax.

"Hey Mengershausen, be careful of this one. It's not right," Castleman called in to his robot driver.

But it was too late. My world erupted in thunder and hate and confusion, ears cleaved from my skull. A shock wave threw me to the ground and overwhelmed my senses and capacity to reason. A cloud of choking dust swept by and chunks of concrete fell about us, hailstones that bounced off my helmet and the top of the Humvee. Did we get hit by a mortar? Rocket-propelled grenade? An accidental detonation of one of our explosive tools? I shook my head and tried to get up and found I couldn't stand. It was only when a robot tire came bouncing toward us, like a child threw it in a game, rolling between our armored truck and the next, that I understood.

I learned later that Mengershausen had tried to wedge his robot gripper under the leading lip of the concrete block, to flip it and examine its soft underbelly. Was it the lifting action? The pushing? We never found out.

When the IED detonated twenty yards away it tore the four-hundred-pound robot to pieces, mangled it beyond recognition, leaving only the rear stump of an amputated arm and a single set of knobby tracks behind. The blast sent molten metal fire and jagged rock in all directions, blowing out the windows and tires of the soft-skinned Iraqi Police trucks and peppering the broadside of our armored Humvee. Keener and

Mengershausen were safe from the frag in the truck. Castleman had taken cover behind the engine block when he recognized the danger of the fake trigger mechanism. By luck or unconscious habit I had kept the bulk of the Humvee's cab between me and the IED; only my shins and the top of my head were exposed.

I calmly patted down my legs and boots and was amazed to find no blood. I tried to stand again and found myself only slightly steadier. All about me our security was suddenly energized, the platoon sergeant barking orders for his turret gunners to wake up and scan rooftops for gunmen. The Iraqi Police huddled to the side confused, except for the weaselly mustached detective who had cut off the hoax black box. He waved his arms in the air and wailed that he was stupid and suicidal and would never walk up to a bomb again.

I raised my rifle to my cheek and looked through my optics across the river and into the slums. The site picture bounced violently. I checked my grip and arm placement; every muscle remembered where to go. Why can't I get a steady shot? I latched on to the rifle tighter, but still I couldn't settle it. I took a deep breath, just as I was taught, and tried again. The red dot danced from riverbed to sky.

"Hey Captain, you okay?" called Castleman, checking and confirming the safety of the team.

"Yeah, I'm good," I called back.

"You sure," he said again, and pointed at my leg.

I looked down. My left leg was bucking and shaking uncontrollably, twitching like a dead animal in its death throes. I willed my leg to be still, but it was possessed and the wild spasms continued unabated. No wonder I couldn't shoot and could barely stand. As the physical symptoms of the coursing adrenaline took over, my veins began to boil. Detachment yielded to anger, shock to bloodlust. They tried to fucking kill me. Fuck them. Fuck this place. We're going home.

I raised my rifle and scanned rooftops again, but smartly no silhouettes remained after the detonation. I wanted a target, somewhere to vent my frustration and powerlessness, but none appeared. The weapons of our security stayed quiet too, and an odd silence settled as it became clear the booby trap was not a signal for ambush.

"I'm going down," announced Castleman.

"The fuck you are," answered Keener.

"I am. Someone has to clear it and we don't have another robot. Get the bomb suit. Put it on me. I'm doing the search for secondaries alone and then we're going to get the fuck out of here."

The Long Walk. Armor on, girded with breastplate and helm and leggings and collar. Eighty pounds of mailed Kevlar. No one can put on the bomb suit alone; your brother has to dress you, overalls pulled up, massive jacket tucked, earnest in his careful thoroughness. One last check, face shield down, and then into the breach alone.

There is no more direct confrontation of wills between bomber and EOD technician than the Long Walk. Donning the suit, leaving behind rifle and security, to outwit your opponent nose to nose. The lonely seeking of hidden danger. To ensure no more hazards lie in wait to snatch the next soldier to pass that way, the next EOD brother or sister, the next local shopkeeper or taxi driver or child playing in a garbage-laden sewer.

No one takes the Long Walk lightly. Only after every other

option is extinguished. Only after robots fail and recourses dwindle. The last choice. Always.

But when the choice comes, when the knife's edge between folly and reason finally tips, training affords a decisiveness to guide your higher purpose. Castleman went so Keener didn't have to. So Mengershausen didn't have to. So I didn't have to. You take the Long Walk for your brother's wife, your brother's children, and their children, and the line unborn.

No greater love does one brother have for another than to take the Long Walk.

Tadasana. Uttanasana. Chaturanga Dandasana. Urdhva Mukha Svanasana. Adho Mukha Svanasana. Tadasana.

Tadasana. Uttanasana. Chaturanga Dandasana. Urdhva Mukha Svanasana. Adho Mukha Svanasana. Tadasana.

And Chair. I shake, from high extended fingertip through outstretched arm, chest full of the Sounding Breath, hips and quivering thighs, down to the end of my toes. The *vinyasa* evolves, flows from *Adho Mukha Svanasana* to *Virabhadrasana.* Warrior.

I am Warrior and my Om and my free mind. My Crazy has melted under the radiant *vinyasa.* I am Warrior from all ages. But I am also Warrior without my rifle. It lies discarded and forgotten. I am the river and I let it go.

"Now we move to Tree," the Yogini says. "Root yourself into the ground. Spread your toes wide. Lift your leg. Hands to prayer position."

I lift my right leg up, and try to push it into my inner left thigh. I stumble the first time, and try again.

"Do not judge yourself," the Yogini says. "If you have trouble balancing, note it and throw it away. If you easily balance, notice and let it go."

I lift my leg again, and retake the position. I press harder, and this time it holds. I stare ahead, a spot on the wall unmoving, and place my hands. I sway. I hold. My vision starts to swim as my eyes grow unfocused and inward. Outward.

"Root yourself to the floor, the rock beneath our feet," says the Yogini. "Feel your Om pass silently out of you and in you."

I am my Om. My Om is not mine. I let it go.

"Open yourself to sight," says the Yogini. "Feel your Third Eye Chakra open on your forehead. Allow yourself to see. Let go of what you see."

I am Tree. My roots are deep. My trunk is slender. My arms are above my head. I sway. I stare into the void.

Spinning and swirling and profound depth. My Third Eye opens. The gray hairy spider crawls out of my forehead and never comes back.

IX | *The Foot in the Box*

THERE WAS SOMETHING about the number one hundred. No one liked getting to a hundred missions. You might not start counting right away, but after a month or two most would go back and make the tally. Seventeen IEDs. Twelve post-blast investigations. Seven weapons caches, buried in dirt floors of crumbling houses. Thirty-six missions. Then, a month later, fifty-three. Sixty-eight. Eighty-seven. As the counter kept clicking up, as you closed in on a hundred, the always-present stomach rumble that came with leaving the FOB gate now grew in intensity. The milestone of one hundred held no particular significance, except that it indicated you had been working too long and soon your luck would run out.

In EOD culture, the role of Chaos is personified in the minor deity Murphy, of the popular Murphy's Law: anything that can go wrong will. Murphy is invoked as a force of random failure by even the most hardened EOD operator to explain any chance occurrence that conspires to kill him or hamper his mission. Ropes that inexplicably loosen or snap. Blasting caps that fail to detonate the plastic explosives they are encased in. Robot batteries dying prematurely despite having been charged the night before. Knives falling from sheaths.

Gear coming up missing from prepacked and inventoried bags. Flat tires and cracked brake lines. A bomb suit's cooling fan breaking only in the worst of the summer heat. In training, Murphy bred annoyance and frustration. In combat, Murphy killed.

An EOD technician learns to respect Murphy at a young age. Like Vikings slaughtering a goat to the sea gods before an expedition to secure good sailing luck, students about to take their final exams in the Ground Ordnance Division of EOD school leave sacrifices and gifts before a totem of Murphy, a wooden pole stuck in the ground with a gorilla mask perched on top. As per tradition, the offerings were cases of beer, cartons of cigarettes, and piles of porno magazines. A purported pragmatic reasoning exists to explain this form of sacrifice, as it was the instructors about to observe and grade your practical test who discreetly snatched up the early-morning presents. I doubt that this ceremony, replayed every couple of weeks when each class completed the division, actually made a bit of difference; my instructors were too bitter and cynical to be easily distracted by smokes and a fresh pair of tits. Still, the psychological benefit for the student was unmistakable. It gave a false impression of control over the random.

But no such offerings can be made in combat, and eventually luck runs out. For luck is the only true defense against Murphy. With each passing mission your luck stretches further and further, allowing Murphy's power to grow. The odds say Murphy always wins in the end. There is no true appeasement. My lucky streak will eventually snap. The only question is whether I will make it home first.

Off again on my new civilian job, training another anonymous EOD unit, in another faux combat town, planting death for the soldiers to discover. Jimbo and JB and John and I are storytellers, traveling bards, spinning a tale of success from unit to unit across the country. Learn these steps, operate these robots, use these explosives, and you too can disassemble the IED, catch the bad guy, and come home a hero. In our training, fighting a pretend war on a training range, the EOD unit always finds the evidence, makes the intel link, unearths the terrorist. And as in a bad television sitcom, all problems are resolved by the end of the weeklong show. Not like when Jimbo and John and I were all deployed. Not like when we burned down the villages, searched the bomb maker's house hours after he had left, combed the countryside for months fruitlessly searching for the nameless foe killing our friends. Not like that. We write the story now, and in our version, the EOD guys win.

But not tonight.

I'm in the basement of a bombed-out apartment complex, built in the Army post's training area in the 1990s to look like Bosnia. Now it is an adequate substitute for Iraq, the sort of concrete container scattered throughout the globe to house the world's poor. There, in the dripping cellar, I'm setting up.

The EOD unit got intel that a U.S. soldier was captured. They've been looking for him all week. They'll get more intel tonight of where he is being held, and will come to try to rescue him.

You never let yourself get captured. Never. In Balad, Hallenbeck had run a line of det cord with thirty seconds of time fuze from the front seat of the Humvee to the main explosives storage cache in the back. If we had gotten overrun, he'd have blown the whole truck, well over two hundred pounds of bang, with us inside. In Kirkuk, Ewbank kept a stock of grenades by his seat. The first couple were for them. The last three were for us. They cut your head off in Iraq when you get snatched. No way I'd have let my wife and children go through that.

For my training scenario I have a volunteer hostage, one young poor kid, recently enlisted, who doesn't know what he's getting into. He's followed me into the cellar with my toys, eager to play an Army game that isn't real to him yet; it hasn't sunk in what's about to happen.

"Listen to me," I say to him before we get started. "I'm about to duct-tape you to a chair, put a fucking bag on your head, and leave you in the dark in a basement torture chamber. I don't know how long it's going to take for the EOD team to find you. Are you sure you're cool with this?"

He is cool with it. I have no idea how that's possible, but we get started anyway.

The concrete cellar is dark and spartan—chair, table, rat nests, and assorted garbage—with only my flashlight sporadically illuminating the deep pitch. I begin by strapping the hostage to the chair, duct tape around his wrists behind his back. In Iraq they would hang men in this position from hooks attached to the ceiling, the full weight of the body dislocating the shoulders during beatings and abuse. Next I taped his legs to the base of the chair and slipped a pressure-release system behind his back, hidden from view and set to blow if he leaned forward. A cell-phone-triggered device under his seat and taped to the underside of the chair. A third booby trap across his chest.

On the table next to him I lay out my tools. Framing hammer. Pliers. Hand pick and hatchet. Coiled hole saw: ragged spiral teeth attached to a power drill. My young hostage's eyes are getting a little wild. I set up a video camera a few feet away in front of him, an old clunky VHS on a tripod to tape his last moments: begging and the hole saw to the temple. I splash a bucket or two of fake blood—red food coloring and corn syrup that attracts flies—on the floor around him, and splatter the rusting tools. A trip line across the entrance doorway, and I'm nearly set.

"Okay, I'm almost done. Are you ready for the bag?" I ask.

"This is just like Halloween!" he answers, giddy.

Not quite. I duct-tape up his mouth, slip the bloodstained and frayed burlap bag over his head, and ask if he can breathe. A mumble confirms it.

I step back, observe my scene. A bound, gagged, and hooded soldier, covered in explosives, head slumping and apparently bashed in. A grisly work area, a nightmare painting across walls and floor and saw, a foot in the box, and the tools of confession. I've transported suburban Baghdad to the United States.

I turn off my flashlight and ink swallows my victim.

The hostage and EOD team should be dead by the end of the night.

Most of the post-blast investigation missions we ran in Kirkuk fell into one of two camps: attacks on U.S. convoys or car bombs set for prominent civilian targets. The roadside IEDs that plagued our patrols and long-haul missions often struck on the open highway between towns or on the boulevards and plazas of the inner cities. The schools, day cares, government ministries, police stations, marketplaces, regime officials' compounds, and hospitals that saw the lion's share of the car-bomb strikes had to be readily accessible by vehicle and thus were often wide, public spaces. The terrain was gruesome, but not claustrophobic.

Not so the scene at the chai shop in the rabbit warrens of northern Kirkuk.

Keener drove our armored Humvee until it ran out of room in the back alleys of the confusing tenement maze. Our U.S. security was lost as well, so many were the twists and turns, false paths, and dingy sewer trails. Kurdish *peshmerga* led us in; not the average Iraqi Police, who as Shiite Arabs were not trusted in this section of town. Sometimes a narrow *pesh* Hilux pickup passed through an opening our Humvees could not and we were forced to reverse course and retreat to another more open fork. This was no place for a firefight. If we got ambushed and needed to leave we wouldn't be leaving quickly.

When the trail became too tight even for Kurdish pickups, Castleman and I dismounted and followed our guide into a maze of covered markets and shops half buried at the base of the crowded concrete apartments that rose like cliff walls around us and smothered the neighborhood. I looked at Castleman, and he looked at me, and we both checked our rifles before we ducked our heads and descended into the dim cavern.

The tunnel-like nature of the market had ensured the death of many. I stepped over broken benches, ripped and torn merchandise, and ankle-deep sticky puddles of people for a hundred meters before we got to the chai shop itself. In the narrow covered confines the blast wave had echoed and reverberated, bounced and doubled back on itself and multiplied until it produced a freight train of agony that scoured this path red. Worse, the chai shop itself had plate-glass windows separating the kitchen and brewing area from public space where patrons sat on benches and at tables to sip their tea. I saw little shattered glass on the ground; I assumed most of it was now at the hospital, embedded in victims.

Castleman spotted a slight depression in the concrete floor

where the IED had been placed. So small a dent, so small a device, so much damage in such an enclosed place. The target was a meeting of Kurdish elders, old men with long beards who sat here each morning with their tea and discussed their troubles, and the troubles of their families, and the troubles of their people. The device was disguised, probably in a plastic crate or a tomato can or olive-oil tin. All of the elders died, as did the workers at the chai shop and the shoppers and vendors at the few market stalls I passed on my way in. I never got a full body count. Fifteen? Twenty?

Castleman and I searched for evidence, pieces of the bomb, but it quickly proved useless. The *pesh* had evacuated the scene and stood respectfully back, but there was little left to grab. Even the discarded body parts of the victims were mostly liquefied—an unidentifiable organ here, half a scalp there, but mostly a ruddy smear across the ceiling, walls, and floor of the concrete market tube.

An eerie quiet permeated, unfamiliar to our ears. I noticed an erect table to one side, out of place among the destruction, with an intact cardboard box on top. The box had to have been put there after the detonation; there was no way it could have survived the blast intact. I looked inside, and did not know immediately what I saw. The thing, it had been human at one time, or at least part of one. There was a sandal, but the flesh inside of it didn't bear any resemblance to a body part I knew. At the top the thing was flayed, opening like a meat flower, muscle petals and a bone central stigma. At its base was a purple engorgement, and this lumpy bag was stuffed into straining leather straps, ten pounds in a five-pound bag.

Was that a foot, in the sandal? I peered closer, and got my first whiff as flies started to buzz around me. I found toenails on the lumpy bag, and a tuft or two of hair, and eventually counted five protrusions. That made the upper splayed-open portion a leg, or the former lower half of one. I eventually found something I would call a tibia and fibula and charred calf muscle in the surrounding skin, holding the mass together in a hollow open cone.

Yes, I had figured it out. It was definitely a foot lying in this cardboard box.

A foot in a box.

Someone had put a foot in a box. I laughed. I couldn't help it. They must have found the foot at the scene, and stuck it in the box for safekeeping. It makes sense, right? Why not put the foot in the box?

I called over to Castleman to look, to show him the joke, but he was distracted by a conversation with our terp and a Kurdish witness. Oh well, his loss.

"Does anyone know how this foot got in the box?" I called out. But few of the *pesh* knew much English, and with our terp otherwise engaged, I got mostly blank stares back. Never mind.

I took a picture of the foot in the box to save for the report. The guys at headquarters in Baghdad would get a kick out of it.

Before I walked away from the table I looked down at my own foot. My formerly tan boots were darkly stained halfway up to the laces, a consequence of doing missions like this one. Buried in those laces on the right boot I had a dog tag: my name, Social Security number, branch of service, blood type, and religious affiliation so they could find me a Catholic priest at the end. Up around the top of each of my boots I had written NKA and O+ in dark black permanent marker: a directive to the medic working on me that I had no allergies and what blood to give me so the priest would not be required.

You put this information on boots because feet survive detonations. They pop off and live to tell the tale, though the rest of you ceases to exist. If I was at the chai shop, I would be a victim, but at least I would not be nameless, like this foot in this box. If I was at the chai shop, they would know it was part of me they were putting in the ground. If I was at the chai shop . . . I looked at the box again.

How easily my own foot slips into that box.

The foot sat in the box. My foot sat in the box.

I stopped laughing. No. No, it's not. It's not my foot in the box. My foot is staying where it is. Whole and recognizable and pink and warm and intact. I'm alive. I'm not scared of the soft sand. I'm living behind my weapon.

I checked my rifle. I'm not scared of the soft sand.

Fuck this place. Fuck that foot in the box. I'm going home.

I have a picture of the dead suicide bomber, sitting upright in the driver's seat of the small silver car, brain smeared across the window, a black hole in his head.

I have a picture, but I don't *need* a picture, you understand. I see the hole in his head right now. I've memorized every speck of dust clinging to his eyelashes. I could relate every detail today.

"How do you remember everything?" my wife asks, as she stands over my shoulder while I type this book. She has noted the lack of research, journals, annotations, personal effects, and mementos piled on the writing desk.

"You can't remember the children's first words. You can't remember them being born, family vacations, or preschool graduation. How do you remember all of this, to be able to go back and write it all down now?" my wife asks again, frustration and emotion in her voice.

I don't try to remember. I don't need to. I'm surrounded by reminders; the images simply emerge in the front of my thoughts. I'm not talking about trite, superficial reminders, like fireworks at the Fourth of July. Oh, to be startled at fireworks again! That is so temporary. The same for the slamming of car doors, or spotting bags and tires on the side of the road, appearing as IEDs on Interstate 90.

It's the small, everyday reminders that are insidious. The rumble of a diesel engine. The smell of gasoline. A large tin can of tomatoes. Traffic circles. Putting on a life jacket. Lacing up a pair of winter boots. Unrolling a sleeping bag.

I'd just as soon forget it all. Replace a dead body or two with a birthday party. But I can't, not while I'm surrounded by the war every day.

When dressing my son before his hockey games, I am always careful with the gear, with each legging, each strap and buckle. But today is special, and I am particularly deliberate for the big game, the championship in Mite Hockey.

First, the cotton socks and undergarments. Then the padded shorts, plates covering his thin thighs, and his skates, extra tight, around the back of his ankle, double-knotted in front, just as he likes. Next, the large, bulky goalie pads, with their complicated laces around the skate blade housing. Then a series of nylon braces and clips along the back of his leg. He looks so skinny, patiently lying on the locker-room floor while I meticulously check each fitting point. Not only are his slight legs swallowed by the wide pads, but his chest and arms are covered only by a tight shirt, accentuating the contrast. Next the puffy upper-body protector, insulated sleeves, and jersey overtop. The final step is the helmet. I start crying as I place it on his head, cinch down the chin cup, and close the cage over his face.

The tears come all the time now. Bedtime stories, movies, the Olympics, news events, and long-form NPR radio pieces, a discordant and unassociated conglomeration of triggers. But those tears are usually in private, in my home, my car, in my son's bed, snuggled up with his back to me so he can't see. These tears, on the other hand, the ones currently blurring my vision, are in the locker room at the arena, and in front of the other children, parents, and coaches, with no filter of privacy. My Crazy is running down my face for all to see.

I've developed some strategies for this kind of moment. You can rub your nose and pull out your handkerchief like you have allergies or a cold. That sometimes works. Or you can make a show of cleaning your glasses, and try to throw in a discreet wipe of the eyes. But under no circumstances can you speak, because your voice will catch and the game will be up. You will be forced to explain why you are crying while putting on your son's goalie equipment.

I just put my seven-year-old son in a bomb suit and sent him on the Long Walk.

Everyone deals with it differently. Many of my brothers that have come home get angry. Angry at themselves. Angry at the world.

I can see it on Bill's face as we stand in line together at the grocery checkout. The store is crowded and busy, and the consolidated feeder line wraps back on itself twice before arriving at our place in the queue. Children cry and tug at their mother's sleeve to buy them a candy bar. A teenage girl talks loudly on a cell phone about some upcoming event and which of her friends will be attending. At one nearby register, a retiree has created congestion by asking the checkout girl to call a manager regarding the use of a particular coupon. The line has not moved in four minutes.

Bill's jaw is set, his knuckles white on the shopping-cart handle. I can see the rage behind his eyes. How can everyone not realize all of the time we are wasting here? Just tell your kids to shut up! They don't need a candy bar. They should be happy there is food on the table. And who cares about the coupons? Are these the problems you have in your life? Candy bars and coupons and who is going to be at the school dance?

The line is a target for a suicide bomber. The line is sucking precious minutes away from his life. All of these little people and all of their little problems. They don't understand what real problems are, or how precious are the minutes that they thoughtlessly dribble away.

"How can you be so calm?" Bill asks as we stand unmoving.

"Why shouldn't I be? It won't make the line move faster," I respond.

"Don't you get angry at how fat and ignorant they all are?" Bill presses.

"I'm not angry. I'm jealous," I say. "I remember when I was ignorant. That was better."

I admire Bill for being angry. When you're angry, you still care. You're still passionate, and engaged, and find meaning in righting a wrong. The line reminds Bill that life is too precious to waste in trivial things.

Not me. The incessant chattering and self-importance of the line reminds me of the priceless ignorance I lost. It reminds me of what I previously considered a problem. Would I graduate from EOD school? Would I get a chance to go back to Iraq and redeem myself? The line reminds me that now I'm just a stupid Crazy vet with a blown-up brain. I'm jealous of the unaware masses I stand with.

When you are Crazy, it's not the war movies, or fireworks, or the nightly news that bother you, as the unafflicted often think. It's the thoughts that come unbidden from grocery lines.

When I get sick of standing in a grocery line, I make a detailed plan to kill those I am surrounded by, allowing me to leave the store.

When I get sick of standing in a grocery line, I'm reminded life is a futile drudgery, and then it will end.

Even now I can see Ewbank's laughing face, streaked brown from the swirling dust stuck to his dripping sweat, as the gunfire opened up in the downtown roundabout. The whistles and pings filled the air, followed shortly by the answering thump-thump of our security's .50-caliber machine gun. Ewbank laughed through it all.

"Civilian life, sir!" Ewbank yelled at me over the din. "It lacks punctuation!"

In World War I they called it shell shock. In Vietnam they called it the thousand-yard stare. In World War II they didn't talk about it at all.

The name that best describes what I feel comes from the Civil War: Soldier's Heart. In 1871, Jacob Mendes Da Costa published his report on three hundred veterans who complained of "irritable heart." The colloquialism "Soldier's Heart" was soon born, and remained in popular usage until the early twentieth century. Da Costa's Syndrome, the official new name for the disease, consisted of palpitations, left-side pain, swelling of the chest, breathlessness, mental distraction, and a reduction in physical endurance and lust for life. Dr. Da Costa attributed the disorder to the prolonged wearing of heavy, restrictive gear, overtight straps on black powder bags, and packs carrying spare clothes and food. Since the Civil War, a soldier's physical load has only grown more burdensome, though the mental toll is timeless.

Today we call it Post-Traumatic Stress Disorder. PTSD. That's what the Crazy feeling is. My Old Counselor has just diagnosed it so.

Now that I have a verdict, a documented disorder, my Old Counselor is energized. I need a shrink. I need the mental-health clinic. I need a month-long retreat in a rehab facility in the country. Most of all, I need drugs.

The wheels of the VA kick into overdrive. My Old Counselor works the phones. She has an emergency PTSD case. Can I be seen right away? Yes, an emergency walk-in. She is going to escort me now.

We rush out of her fussy closet office to the patient transport elevators segregated for hospital staff priority use. To the tenth floor my Old Counselor hurries me, arm in arm, past the check-in window, past the waiting room filled with hushed sad faces, to a back office where my New Shrink awaits.

"Thank you so much for seeing him right away," my Old Counselor says, out of breath from the rushed transfer.

"He has PTSD and I am very concerned," my Old Counselor repeats, several times.

The blond woman at a small desk decorated with green house plants slowly turns from the computer screen she had been reviewing. She smiles at me, a serene, reassuring smile.

"We'll take a look at him, thank you," my New Shrink says as she leads my Old Counselor from the office, easing her out with a slowly closing door.

A quiet stillness settles over the blue, airy office with the click of the door latch. My New Shrink, younger, calmer, gestures for me to sit near her desk. I take a deep breath, sit in the chair, and await my sentence.

"Brian," my New Shrink begins, "why do you think you're here?"

"Because I'm Crazy. And because my Old Counselor says I need drugs." I thought this was self-evident.

"Do you think you need medication?" she asks.

"I don't know if I need them. I know I don't want them."

"Why not?"

"I'm scared. I'm scared to not be myself. I'd rather be Crazy than be someone else."

"Well, you aren't Crazy," my New Shrink gently corrects. "We don't use that word here. Are you going to kill yourself, Brian?"

No one has ever asked me that before. I have to really think about it.

"No, I don't think so. Maybe before, but I'm not going to now."

"Then, if you aren't going to kill yourself, I'm not going to prescribe anything today either," my New Shrink says.

"You're not?"

"No," she says. "I'll respect your wish for now. Until we aren't able to make progress without them. Until there is no other way."

She turns toward her computer, pulls up my chart, and briefly scans the various cardiac tests I've had, my regular visits to the ER, the months with the Old Counselor endlessly rehashing Jeff, and Kermit, and rifles, and the hole in the bomber's head. She looks back at me with a hint of sadness.

"Tell me, Brian," she begins, "about the day you lost all

hope, saw your foreshortened future, and realized life had no meaning."

Metallic airport terminals, a succession of fast-food peddlers and superficial bookstores, consistent and interchangeable. Dulles, O'Hare, Charlotte. Same restaurants. Same newspapers, piled on wooden stands outside the same convenience stores. Same rushing businessmen, flight attendants and pilots, young families, and visiting Chinese tourists.

I swim against this sea regularly, on my way from one EOD unit to another, training another deploying crew, a repeated timeless cycle on a grueling schedule. The airports have melded into a blur; plug-and-play passengers, overpriced burritos. My layovers are on autopilot, endured to the next flight.

But once in a while, my subconscious notes an anomaly.

A tingle on the nerves that something is different, a fly in the soup of the otherwise homogeneous and busy crowd.

I've been walking from one terminal to the next, burning off adrenaline, bypassing the automated walkways, taking the stairs up and down, working up a sweat under my coat and flannel shirt. The Crazy feeling won't let me sit at a gate anymore, and with a long layover, my wanderings have taken me farther afield. I pace in a cloud of my overactive mind's self-reflections and distractions until that nerve tingle pushes aside the muddled haze. I come alert to find myself in the international terminal, at the gate of Ethiopian Airlines and a flight bound for Addis Ababa.

I scan the waiting travelers, to find the source of my unbidden arousal. Which one of these is not like the others? Dark East African families with children, lighter Somali graduate students, white European businessmen with multinational firms. Everyone and everything is in place. Everyone, except for the three trim men sitting a bit to the side, backs to the wall, trying to blend in. They may be innocuous to most, but to anyone who does the job, they might as well have a strobe light above their heads.

Their team leader is older than me by a couple of years, short brown hair graying slightly, all khaki safari shirt and cargo pants, high-end hiking boots. His Oakley sunglasses are perched on his head, his watch face covers almost his entire wrist, and the laptop on his knees came out of a black, hardened, over-engineered waterproof case. His two companions, one black and one white, share the athletic physique, the overpriced sunglasses, the choice in footwear. But both are younger, listening to iPods, assault packs tossed at their feet. Beards are starting on all their faces—the call for the job must have been last minute. All appear ready to run five miles uphill at a moment's notice. Contractors. Mercenaries. Like me, but going overseas, for more money, most likely for a three-letter agency. Ethiopia is probably not their final destination. Somalia? Sudan?

The leader looks up from his laptop, charade put aside for the moment, and faintly nods in my direction. I nod back. Their rifles materialize at their feet, a desert mirage, propped among their backpacks and gear, pistols tucked in drop holsters on their legs. I can feel the familiar grip of my rifle in my hand. The comforting grooves on the bolt-release paddle on my left thumb, the heavy satisfying *thunk* as the spring is released, the bolt moves forward, and the round slides into the chamber. A deep breath. I wonder if they need a fourth man on the team. What's the job? Personal security detail? Door kickers? Every stack needs a bomb technician.

I think about going back every day. Back to the job. Back to the clarity of thought, the singleness of purpose, the mundane details of the world falling away and only the essential remaining. No bills. No to-do lists. No children asking for attention. No tear-filled marital counseling with my wife. No broken lawnmower and early-morning soccer practice and dentist appointments to schedule. No clutter.

For a moment, I do more than just consider going back. The helo inserts, rifle slung and feet dangling out the side, legs kicking in the breeze. The cordon-and-search assaults, knocking on a door in the middle of the night, lighting a valley on fire with thousands of pounds of explosives. The Crazy purrs its approval.

The safe and familiar and comfortable beckon. Why not go back? To where life makes sense, and I'm good at what I do.

Maybe someday, but not today. My flight will be leaving soon. I need to get back to my gate. The man in khaki catches my eye, nods one more time, and then looks away down the concourse. I follow his gaze that has perked up, and the Spidey sense tingles again.

First a stare, from a businessman standing outside the gate. Then a watchful eye from a couple in a lounge across the way. I catch a glance. They look away. An awareness floods me, surges from my groin and drowns my brain.

I'm in danger. I'm alone, isolated, surrounded and suffocated by the crowd. I need to egress, violently if necessary. Avoid a static direct firefight. Shoot, move, and communicate. Live behind your weapon. Do whatever is required to go home.

I grasp my rifle, which has been waiting for me at my shoulder. I need to leave this airport terminal right now. I need to get out.

The closest emergency exit is two gates down, on the left. I know because I've scouted the area before, part of my regular contingency planning. I should be able to get there in less than a minute. As my right hand settles into its familiar position on my carbine's pistol grip, elbow bent, wrist fully turned, index finger above and outside of the trigger guard, I choose my targets. The main transit security force is in the next concourse, and I don't see a roaming cop between me and the door. The female airline staff personnel manning the gate will duck and run. The crowd of sheep blocking me from the exit are helpless, except for a few.

The man in the suit thirty meters ahead spends a lot of time in the gym. He is taller and stronger than I am. He is the biggest threat, and is in my way. He should be first. I grip my rifle tighter, and pick up my pace.

Next is the teenager, just past him, with the navy high-school football T-shirt. His slight father next to him will cower, but he won't. I'll have to kill him too.

I count the rounds in my rifle magazine. I visualize the first two into the chest of the man in the suit, the frightened reaction of the crowd, the next two through the football player. I visualize stepping over them to the exit. The foot sits in the box on the counter at the next gate. My breath is coming faster now, as I begin to make my move. My blood is pounding in my ears, my heart strong, quick and regular, the typical gurgling and skipping corrected and overcome. I prepare to drop the first target. I need to get out of this terminal.

I quicken my pace. Ten meters to the first mark, twenty-five to the emergency exit.

I put my finger on the trigger. I am going to make it home.

The man in the suit catches me staring at him. Square in the eye.

Goddamn it.

I stop, self-consciously pause, then turn away. I know the look I have on my face.

What the fuck am I doing?

It's happening again. I thought it would have gone away by now.

Ashamed, I awkwardly shuffle out of the main concourse thoroughfare, mumbling apologies, head down, looking away. I place my back to the wall, between the Nuts on Clark stand and the woman trying to get me to fill out a credit-card application. My heart is pounding out of my chest, and the Crazy is in my throat. Desperate, I reach for my cell phone, and dial my wife as quickly as I can.

"I'm doing it again." I skip even saying hello.

"What are you doing? Aren't you supposed to be on a layover?" she says.

"I'm picking people to kill." Tears come unbidden.

There is a pause at the other end of the line.

"It's your anniversary, you know," my wife says.

I had forgotten, but I know which one she is referring to. I got home two years ago today.

"You're always worse on an anniversary," she says.

She's right. I wish I knew why.

"I don't like being like this. Normal people don't do this. Planning to kill random strangers."

"Just go to your plane, and you'll be fine. We'll talk when you get home. Are you okay now?" she asks.

No.

"Sure," I say instead. She hangs up.

Breathe, Brian. Breathe.

I pick my head up, and re-see a harmless crowd, the anonymous normalcy, the unthreatening busyness.

The young dark-haired woman from the credit-card kiosk walks up to me. "You could earn twenty-five thousand miles by applying for a new platinum card today," she coos.

I put my rifle down and head to Gate C23.

I looked for Ricky on my run today, but he wasn't there to meet me. He didn't say he was coming, but I expected him. We run together most days now. It's nice to have a brother on the run, to help me through the uphill sections, encourage me when I need to dig in, dig deeper.

But Ricky wasn't there, so I ran alone. Overcast sky, blustery headwind, a struggle from beginning to end. The Crazy boiled the whole way, barely waning at the height of my exertion. I returned troubled, alone.

It is now evening, darkness coming quickly in the early winter, and I sit on the mattress in my bedroom at home, eyes closed, my wife and children downstairs. I breathe like my New Shrink has been trying to teach me. Mindful of my breath. Mindful of my presence. Being present, simply in the breath.

My mind re-creates the yoga forms. Then they too blur, a stillness comes over me, and my mind is blank.

Silence in the room, the clatter from the house shut out. With each breath, I feel the Crazy deflate, compact, coalesce, first into my gut, and then lower, further compressing, passing down and out. I sense an incredible emptiness in my chest, a blessed smallness.

My Crazy is still. For the first time in over half a year, my Crazy is extinguished. Not smothered with pain, or burned to evaporation, but gone. It returns a minute later, a bubbling rise, but for a moment, there was nothing.

I can beat this.

Maybe outside of my head there is an objective reality. At peace.

x | *Ricky*

WE HAD NO front line in our war. A front line only exists when two standing armies look over a field at one another. Our army didn't do much standing, and we were fighting the ever-changing sea we swam in. But we didn't swim continuously. We stepped into and out of that sea; the front gate of the FOB was the shore, and there I turned the switch on and off.

Out in the city, on the highway, in the helicopter, danger lurked everywhere. No smiling locals, no pile of trash, no abandoned parked car could be trusted. Your brain was always on, your back never turned, your rifle always ready, finger on the trigger.

But once we got back to the FOB, back to the HAS, a two-foot-thick concrete dome sheltered your righteous head from that crashing sea. The vest came off, the rifle was set down, the breath came easier. A take-out dinner from the chow hall and a cigarette and a laugh around the fire pit outside with your brothers. Back inside the gate, you were safe again.

And so every day the pendulum swung. Danger to safety. Safety to danger. As the missions piled up, getting back to the HAS took on new urgency. It was bad luck to die at all, but getting schwacked with three weeks left, two weeks left, one

week, would be the height of tragedy. Eventually the end of
the deployment was in sight, and we counted the days until
there were no more missions, no more trips off the FOB, no
more forays into danger. The goal was to go home, because if
the HAS was safe, home was Safe.

He drove the robot down to the hidden device, camouflaged
with trash and debris, on the side of the windblown highway
on the south end of Kirkuk. The worst of the summer heat had
broken, but that only reduced the temperature from broil to
bake, and the sun still oppressed. While Mengershausen stared
at the robot screen, I kept one eye on the crowd gathered to
watch and one eye on our security.

"Hey, watch your sector, not us!" I shouted over to the gunner atop the nearest Humvee.

Our security was new, green, fresh off the plane. They couldn't
run logistics convoys without getting shot, they couldn't go
on patrol without getting blown up, and if they did accidentally stumble across an undetonated IED in a stroke of luck,
they couldn't tell us where it was so we could clear it. It took
an hour of searching to find this one; we eventually had to
call in helos to scout the road ahead. They discovered it hundreds of meters away from the initially reported spot. Clocks
ticking as they ran out of fuel, the mini Kiowa helicopters
eventually flew right up next to the thing and dropped smoke
grenades on it. Ten feet off the deck, tipped on their side, the
pilot popped and tossed the purple canister out the window,
rotor wash churning up the surrounding desert, each blade tip
inches from the road.

The infantry brigade in place when we arrived—which had
shown us the ropes, driven and flown us everywhere, and pro-

tected our teams on every mission—had reached the end of their tour, packed up, and gone home. The new brigade was just that, and this kid manning the turret gun looked like he had only been in the Army since breakfast. We served as the overlap, the continuity, and were suddenly the old veterans and voice of wisdom. Not that it mattered much; the new brigade seemed determined to relearn every lesson the hard way. Casualties were way up, and my morale was just as far down. I didn't have the time or patience to teach a whole brigade how to survive their tour. I certainly didn't have the faith or goodwill to let them figure it out by experimenting with me. Let the helo drivers pick up their slack, we weren't going to echo it. Home was too close to start fucking around with newbie security teams now.

"I'll let you know before we blow anything up, don't worry," I yelled up again. "You look for bad guys and let us worry about the IED!"

I almost felt bad for the new brigade. We were leaving too. They'd unknowingly pay for our mistakes, and those of the brigade they replaced—for every cordon and search of the wrong house, farmer's burned field, flex-cuffed innocent, and pock-marked road. But we had paid for the unknowable actions of those that came before us as well. EFP and car-bomb retaliations as revenge for assaults and firefights forgotten. We paid our due, but not for what we had done. When I left Iraq, the U.S. military had occupied it for five years. But we didn't collectively have five years of experience; we had one year of experience five times. And through it all, the Iraqis endured, and remembered, and resented, and hated the fresh, young, pimple-faced kid sitting on the Humvee near me, though he was in middle school when the first cruise missiles fell on Baghdad.

"Hey, Mengershausen, did you ID the main charge on the end of that command wire yet?"

"Yeah, it's another improvised claymore."

"Rusty cylinder sleeve with nuts and bolts for frag?"

"Yup. Same ones we've been seeing the last month."

"How many is that now since we hit the EFP factory?"

"Sir, I can't even keep up trying to count."

"Did we used to have improvised claymores before we did that botched EFP factory job?"

"Not like this."

"We're pushing our luck. We're too short to get blown up again. Just whack this motherfucker and let's get out of here."

I don't remember which mission was my last. It all gets fuzzy at the end. But one day our replacements arrived, and it was our turn to pick them up in Hiluxes and drive them back to their new home in the HAS. Their arrival portended the certainty that the war would continue without us. And just like that, it's not your job to leave the FOB anymore, not until you get on the airplane bound for home. Your war doesn't end with a climactic battle or a crescendo of missions. It ends with silence; one day the phone just stops ringing. That call you went on yesterday? Turns out that was your final run outside the wire. When the phone rings again, someone else will answer it. Your war is over.

I thought about two things on the flight home: sex and alcohol. The latter was surer than the former; I had to endure my wife's anger at my absence for a long time before we had our homecoming.

The alcohol, on the other hand, flowed freely from the moment we hit non-Muslim soil. Back at the FOB the Special Forces guys always had beer smuggled in via C-130, and they were more than happy to share after missions. But we were always discreet, and it was saved for special occasions. We wanted a proper celebration, a survival celebration: kegs and cigars and naked bodies in the hot tub. It started when the plane landed in Germany. It continued in the wee hours during a quick refueling stop in Iceland. The homecoming party at Luke's house happened two days later, once safely back at Nellis in Las Vegas.

Ricky met me at the door with a giant bear hug. We were on opposite deployment schedules, and so were always around to put each other on the plane and welcome each other back. I had gotten the beer cold for his return eight months prior. Now he was returning the favor.

"It's good to have you back, sir," Ricky said. His skinny arms squeezed with surprising strength.

"It's good to be back, bro," I yelled over the music.

Ricky's wife had already joined a flock of giggling girlfriends in the hot tub, and a game of Strip Jenga was in session at the kitchen table. Q handed me a beer, Grish a cigarette, and we talked and joked and smoked and drank and lied and told war stories and savored life and marveled that the indulgent pleasures of this existence endured. Your brothers saw you off. Your brothers welcomed you back. Your brothers ensured your survival in between.

I made it home. So did everyone else I took to Kirkuk on that trip. We did what we had to do to make sure of it. Our mission was to come home in one piece. That the best way to accomplish this mission was to not go on the call, to never leave in the first place, only occurred to me much later.

I never had to go back to Iraq. And I haven't.

The Army insisted on holding a graduation ceremony, to celebrate the end of our predeployment training at Fort Sill, the last requirement before my trip to Kirkuk. Phillips had to give a speech, as he was the highest ranking officer among us. We were all captains, but he bested me by a couple of months.

Phillips was not excited to give a speech, and I was just as happy the duty didn't fall to me. Still, I thought of what I would say should it come to it. What would I say to my men, this day before we boarded the plane for Iraq? A first trip for some, return trip for most, second trip for me, my chance to redeem myself, to make right my failure my first time around.

I wrote a speech in my head, and never gave it. I wrote it down later that day and saved it, saved the burning need to deploy, saved the drive, saved the choice to live my dream, saved the idealism and the ego, saved the optimism and the duty, for when I would need it later.

"Fellow EOD operators," I wrote. "We are riding the front crest of history. In the sixty years of Air Force EOD, we have never been as busy. We are making history every day.

"Lexington. Concord. Saratoga. Tripoli. Baltimore and New Orleans. Shiloh. Gettysburg. Vicksburg. San Juan Hill. The Ardennes and the Marne. Omaha Beach. Anzio. Pearl Harbor and Midway. Inchon and the Yalu River. Khe Sanh. Da Nang and the Mekong Delta. Panama and Kuwait City.

"These names are written in blood upon the heart of every soldier, sailor, airman, and Marine. These names are burned into our souls. In fifty or one hundred years, when historians write of our current war, new names will be added to that list. Bagram and Kandahar. Baghdad and Baqubah. Kirkuk. Fallujah. And then we will count ourselves lucky to be among those privileged few who can say they played a small part in the continuing honor and legacy of the Armed Forces of the United States. I am humbled to be among the few who can speak to their children and grandchildren about what history will write of us. Cherish this opportunity.

"The bond among EOD brothers and sisters is our greatest strength. That bond will bring us home."

I came home, but then what follows? I never considered. But I chose it all the same.

I haven't seen him since high school, probably graduation night itself. The years have not been kind; more around the middle, less on top, and now a flaccidity to his grip. A droopiness to his face and speech.

"Thank you for coming," he says.

"I wouldn't miss it," I respond. "It was good to see you again. I'm glad there was a great turnout." A turnout to his fundraiser, paying for his medical bills.

He is now the one in the class with Lou Gehrig's disease. It strikes five out of every hundred thousand people. Our class was only two hundred. Because he has it, now I won't. That's how these things work. We both know it, as do the rest of his former classmates that have come to the event. Our donations are thanksgiving sacrifices of gratitude.

I'm standing in an awkward circle of those former classmates, sixteen years since we last saw each other. An accountant, a dentist, a lawyer. One guy has a daughter with leukemia. Another lost his wife in a car accident. I'm the one that's Crazy. I feel better that my wife and kids are now safe from car accidents and leukemia. If they knew, they'd feel better that they aren't going to become Crazy.

We exchange pleasantries and make modest inquiries. What

do you do now? Oh, you work for the bank? Are you married? Children? It is all very harmless and polite until someone innocently asks me my occupation.

"I just got back from Iraq. I disarm bombs."

That was a mistake. Mild shock, wide eyes from a few. Do they not expect it from me personally? Or just not from anyone they might regularly encounter in their lives? The war is very far away from here.

"That sounds terrible. I'm not sure I could do that," says the accountant.

"Oh, it's tons of fun, actually. Now that I lived through it. We've lost a lot of bomb technicians over the last nine years. I'm just really lucky I didn't die."

Nervous laughter from the dentist.

"Hey, but don't worry. I don't blow people up anymore."

Silence.

I know where this is going. At my sister's wedding I cornered the parents of an old friend for an hour, drunk and inappropriate and occasionally crying, painting a detailed study of the pink mist that hangs over a scene after a car bomb explodes, intestines and arms hanging from trees. How the foot was in the box. Because, I mean, really, where else would you put it, if you had a foot no longer attached? In a box! Isn't that hilarious!

I check my rifle. I've learned how to cope now. Time to turn the filter back on.

"But I've still got all my fingers and toes!" I wiggle them for effect—that always seems to work. "So I must have done something right. I'm just happy to be home with my wife and kids. How many kids do you have now? Congratulations. Don't they grow up fast? Oh, I love that age. They're learning so much, and so much fun, and almost ready for school. Enjoy them while you can. My oldest is nearly a teenager, and man, can they eat!"

My thighs and lungs are burning as fiery hot as the cooked desert pavement beneath my feet, the Texas summer robbing me of breath and endurance. But every painful step keeps the Crazy in check for another moment, a blessed delay of the inevitable.

Ricky seems indefatigable and presses on ahead, always a step or two in front so I never quite catch him. I redouble my effort, strain and claw and chase him up over the next rise, finally catching him at the top of the low bluff. The path heads down again, and we settle into an easier rhythm, opening our stride to take advantage of the descent.

"I'm all alone, Ricky," I say to him once I catch my breath.

"What do you mean, sir?" he replies.

"It's tough being out. Not having a unit or the guys around, like when we were stationed together. There are no EOD guys at home in Buffalo. I feel like I don't fit in anywhere. And I travel all the time, teaching, a new city every month. I'm never settled," I say.

"What about your psychologist at the VA?" Ricky asks.

"I'm on my second one!" I say. We laugh and pick up the pace.

"Give her a chance," Ricky says. "And anyway, you've always got me."

"That's true." I pause. "I miss you, bro."

"I know."

At first I felt cheated.

When I got home, I knew the signs to look for, the indicators that one is having trouble readjusting to American life. I even sought out those signs, secretly hoped for at least a few of them. Instead, the bulk of the horrors initially faded, and it was with a drop of regret that I saw them go. I had always heard combat was a life-altering event, and my pride wanted my experience to qualify. If a little jumpiness came with the mark, so be it.

I had needed to go back, and now I needed it to count.

Instead, as the homecoming parties ended, and the hangover faded, and I cut back on the cigarettes, life returned to a surprising normal relatively quickly. After a couple of months home, the slam of a car door no longer made me jump, and I didn't look for IEDs on the side of the road while driving. I left the military, got my civilian job as a trainer, taught EOD technicians without flashbacks or distraction. The vigilance lapsed, comfort returned, and a sigh of relief eventually came unbidden.

Perhaps I don't measure up with those that came before after all, I thought. Perhaps it was only delusion or adrenaline in the moment that led me to believe so. You aren't so special, Brian. This won't be the defining episode you had hoped for.

Time to move on with life. I guess I made it back in one piece.

But I didn't. I had a blown-up brain, a foot in a box, and Crazy lurking around the corner. I just didn't know it yet.

My Crazy was waiting for me, stalking, hiding in the shadows and on the edge of my vision. I see it now, in retrospect. Some old habits that never did go away. Some memories that stayed fresh. Until one day, seemingly out of the blue, it surprised me walking down the street. I stepped off a curb normal. I landed Crazy.

There is no explanation for why I went Crazy when I did. I don't know why that was my day. Nothing had happened. I had been out of the military for over two years. I had been home for even longer. The wars continued without me: brothers deployed, came home, died, survived. Shouldn't I have gone Crazy when Kermit died? When Jeff died? But I didn't. My day was February 6th, in the Pearl District, in Portland, Oregon. The day my chest swelled and never released and my overactive mind eradicated all sensible thought and temperance. The day I went Crazy.

The strangeness of the feeling struck me first, then the discomfort, the unease. I continued up the street, among the trendy shops and bars. My eye was twitching by the time I sat down for dinner in a McMenamins restaurant. Three beers and dinner and the Crazy feeling didn't subside. It followed me to bed in my hotel room, kept me awake past midnight, and then greeted me before dawn. Beyond unsettled, beyond distracted. I took it to work teaching each day for the rest of the week, packed it in my carry-on bag on the airplane, and brought it home. Still the Crazy didn't subside. I twitched and gurgled all the way to the emergency room when I could stand no more.

I don't deserve to be Crazy. Not that I'm too good for it, but rather not good enough. Not enough tours. Not enough missions. Not enough bodies. Not enough IEDs. Not enough near misses. No friend dead in my arms. No lost limbs. No face exploding in my rifle scope. Plenty of other guys did more, endured more, and came home in worse shape. They deserved it, not me.

I'm still scared of the soft sand. I didn't earn Crazy.

What did I assume it would be like, once I came home? A Goldilocks state of solemn pride. Remembering those that came before, telling the story of their valor, a satisfaction in having done my part, and a successful life to follow. A single tear at the Veterans Day parade once a year, and otherwise, dignity and bearing and no more.

I managed no such balance. Instead, I vacillated from breezy inattention to the inescapable rush of Crazy. What I would give for the initial flippancy again.

Emerson was right. Life does consist of what you spend your whole day thinking of. I think of the Crazy all day now, either in the forefront of my mind, or as a shadow that follows me, always there if looked for. The life of the mind used to be a joy but now it is a cursed downward spiral, the Crazy feeding on itself, growing and amplifying unless I run it into the ground or meditate it away. I can't exercise or practice yoga all day, and so the Crazy creeps back, first one intrusive thought, then another, until it writhes again at full boil.

If life is what I think about all day and I'm Crazy all day then my life is now Crazy.

"But I was going to kill those women," I say to my New Shrink. "On the Day of Six VBIEDs."

I can hear their screams in my mind unbidden, breaking my constantly sought peace. The heat, and the dust, and ankle-deep pools of rotting blood and sewage fill my nose. It makes me as angry now as it did then. They never shut up. They still don't shut up. Their cries and mourning have followed me home and into the VA hospital.

"I could have done it," I said. "I was capable of doing it."

Is this a boast or a confession? And am I trying to convince her or myself?

"But you *didn't* do it," my New Shrink soothes. "That's what's important, that you didn't shoot them."

"That's not it," I reply. "The only reason I didn't shoot them is because I wasn't strong enough. I pussed out. I got scared. They were screaming, and I wanted them dead, and I had my rifle and I thought about doing it. But I'm no saint for not pulling the trigger. I would have done it if I wasn't so weak. I'm no better than any of the terrorists we were chasing. They just had the balls to go through with it, and I didn't. They had the will. I wish I did, but I don't."

"It's to your credit that you spared them," my New Shrink insists. "As well as the fact that it bothers you now."

"Over there, the Kurds and Arabs, they hate each other more than they love their own children. But I'm no better. I don't hate them or their children, but I'd kill them all if it brought back Jeff and Ricky."

Ricky died in an operating room in Seattle, two months before I went Crazy.

His brain exploded on a plane from Florida to Washington, traveling with his wife and daughter to visit family. An aneurysm, a flood to his frontal lobe. Released because of the pressure differential in the aircraft? We'll never know. He had a splitting headache on the plane and was nauseous from the pain by the time they landed. Disoriented, confused, mumbling, and no longer speaking English in the car on the way to the hospital. He attacked the medical technician giving him a CT scan in the emergency room, a different person with a different personality. He was unconscious by midnight, and dead the next morning.

It could have been random bad luck. It could have been related to the melanoma he had successfully fought years before. A bit of metastasized tumor released, growing in his brain but randomly disengaged on the flight.

I don't think so. I think it was a remnant of his own traumatic brain injury, a time bomb left dangling on a thread waiting for the right moment to let go. Ricky was on the airborne team, jumped out of planes, and had survived multiple trips to Iraq. He did everything right, paid his dues, lived behind his weapon, made it home, and took a lower-stress, lower-risk job at the EOD school in Florida. Ricky died not in combat, but as a teacher. A teacher on vacation.

They killed him. He made it back from the mission, and back to the FOB, and then back home, and was finally safe. But he wasn't. None of us are. They can still kill us anytime.

I picked up the pace of my race after that.

"Wow," my New Shrink said. "You are on fast-forward."

"Sir, have you ever heard the parable about the jar of marbles?" says Ricky. "About the guy who figured out, based upon his age and average life expectancy, about how much time he had left in his life. He filled a jar with that many marbles and every day took one out. Every day the jar of marbles got emptier. It reminded him of how precious life is. There is too much to do, too much to enjoy and savor. Life is too short to waste on worries and being Crazy."

"That's horseshit, and you know it," I reply. "The day we all got off the plane in Iraq, all of us decided to take our jars of marbles and pour them out all over the floor. We don't have any time left. It's all borrowed from now on. You want a marble analogy? It's more like we dumped ours out, and decided to add a marble every day we lived. But who knows how many you can add? Jeff and Kermit didn't get to add any marbles. And you only got to add a few. Who knows how many I get to add. Today might be the last one. They can still kill me. They still killed you. And every day I look at my jar of marbles and try to decide if I've packed enough in to justify my little pile. And every day the answer is no.

"Ricky, we're all running a race. And I used to think it was a marathon, nice and long and a set distance. That I could plan my race well, knew where the landmarks were, knew where the finish line was, and that by the end I could look back with pride at how I ran.

"But I was wrong. Now I know better. It's not the distance that's set, it's the time. Fate has a clock counting down, and you don't get to see how much time is left. I thought I had time to finish the race. But now I see that if I don't speed up, I'll never make it. I won't get as far as I want. I need to run faster to run farther. Forget the starter's pistol. There is a finisher's pistol, and it could go off at any time."

"You are concentrating so hard on how far you run," says Ricky, "that you have ignored how well you run. Or enjoyed the steps you are taking today. Learn from me. I enjoyed each of my steps. Are you enjoying yours?"

"No," I respond. "Every delay, every moment I spend waiting in a line, at the airport, at a restaurant, makes me Crazier. And every accomplishment gets pushed aside to focus on the next task. This extra time, to put marbles in my jar, is not a gift. It's a curse of knowledge and responsibility. To make each marble worthy. And to put in all the marbles you couldn't."

"You can't run two races, yours and mine," says Ricky. "Mine is done."

"So why then should I take any more steps, if each one is so miserable? Why start in the first place? When I know now what I'm capable of? I have a reason to run faster, Ricky, but not a reason to run at all."

XI | *The Mountain*

THE GENTLE SWAYING of the Humvee had put Ackeret to sleep several hours earlier. He sprawled in the rear seat next to me, head back, mouth open, gently snoring. I could only see him when Trey, sitting in the team-chief seat ahead of us, turned on his dim red tactical light. In the dull glow, Ackeret's dark moustache stood out starkly on his pale face. It was a terrible moustache; thin, spotty, rodentlike. He loved it. I loved telling him how bad it was.

Despite the hour I couldn't sleep. It was the kind of day that was never today, according to Trey's logic. We had never quite made it to our racks when the call came in. We left the FOB after dark, drove the empty highway to clear a crush-switch-initiated artillery round forty klicks away that was blocking a route-clearance mission, and were now headed back. Driving barely faster than a crawl so the lead security vehicle could use its high-power strobe lights to search for hazards, the entire mission would last more than eight hours. Plenty of time for Ackeret to sleep.

I peered again out my window, thick armored glass distorting the view. Not a single light broke the complete darkness; the horizon and sky united in a black wall of undetermined depth. Out the front window, the red running lights of the Humvee we followed were barely visible, obscured by the dust kicked up off the road by our security convoy. Our feeble headlights did little to pierce the gloom; as the clouds of dirt and sand waxed and waned, our view never extended far. Like snow flurries back home, the dust just reflected back at us what little light we gave off. Often we could see no further than the front bumper of our armored truck. The world was all tan and black, darkness and dust; a layer of tan silt covered our tan truck, our tan uniforms and armor, inside and out, lit first by Trey's small lamp, then not at all. Bolger drove often and knew the road well. He just kept us straight and true, unfazed by the fact that he could see the truck in front of us less than half the time.

The world fell completely away, and I could sense nothing beyond the warm rocking cocoon the four of us shared. The hum of the diesel engine. The glint off Trey's rifle, and the racks of 5.56-millimeter magazines hanging from the driver's seat in front of me. The musky communal smell of four men who had missed their last shower. Trey's iPod was playing quietly over the speakers wired into the cab, and he and Bolger were having a whispered conversation at the edge of my hearing, trying to let Ackeret and me sleep. A snore from next to me. A soft laugh from Trey. I smiled.

Cushioned and wrapped in the comforting false security blanket of our truck's armored chassis and the insulating impenetrable dark, my mind wandered. It escaped our dingy capsule and flitted among trivialities, remembered the trifling normality at home. Tucking my children into their beds. Giving them a bath. Setting a morning cup of coffee on the nightstand next to my sleeping wife, waiting for her to wake.

For a moment, I could taste the coffee on my lips, feel my

wife's hand on my hand, smell the clean-washed hair of my just-bathed son.

A gust of wind blew against the side of the truck, and another cloud of dust washed over us, blotting out the world anew. And then, at that moment, a bird flew down silently and perched just in front of us, on the bumper of the Humvee, and looked steadily at me.

It was a pigeon, common gray and completely unremarkable except for the fact that it just landed on the grille of a moving armored truck in a dust storm.

"Holy shit, look at that," Bolger burst out from the driver's seat.

"Trey, don't move," I whispered. The pigeon had landed right in front of him.

"What the fuck," Trey said, laughing quietly, but he didn't move much.

The bird looked at us, readjusted its footing, flapped its wings once, but made no move to fly away. It stayed perched on the brush guard, the metal trim surrounding the headlight, swaying gently with the roll of the road amid the swirling grime.

The world was now the four of us and a pigeon.

"What should we do?" asked Bolger.

"Why do we need to do anything?" I said. "He's not hurting anything."

A respectful silence settled on the truck, the bird content to join us, as we drove slowly through the darkness. I stared at the bird, an eternity passed, and I broke the quiet.

"Trey, what are you going to do when you get home?" I said.

"Probably buy another gun, or fix up my truck. I don't know. I haven't thought about it," Trey said.

"You haven't thought about it?"

"No, this is where I'm supposed to be. I don't do well at home. When I'm there, I dream of being here. We have work to do here. My brothers are here. Who else is going to bring Ackeret's dumb ass back home? No, this is where I'm supposed to be," Trey said, his voice trailing off.

He turned and longingly looked out the window into the night.

"I'll keep coming back as long as they let me," he said softly.

All of a sudden the dust settled around us, falling away as we turned a corner and followed the convoy up onto a fully paved road. Newly exposed, the sky erupted in a canvas of purple and red. The sandy haze now enabled a dramatic color in the predawn sky, stripes of clouds crisscrossing above us and the faintest hint of bluing crown. A single shocking beam of morning's first light leaped from the horizon, and the spell now broken, the bird flapped its wings and disappeared.

Ackeret continued to snore next to me. Nothing woke him.

"We begin our practice today," my Yogini says, "in Mountain Pose. *Tadasana*. Stand fully erect. Shoulders back. Hands at your side. Open your heart. Feel your feet stretch and reach into the ground. Look out over the tip of your nose."

Tadasana.

"Stand in Mountain Pose," my Yogini says, "and breathe."

I root into the ground, fill my lungs, and open my eyes.

The mountain is real. It exists outside of my head. It exists outside of my Crazy. It is objective, innocent, peaceful existence. It is real.

Mountains are real. Forests are real. Rivers and plains and the drift of cloud above me are real. The infinite depth of the

Milky Way and the single blade of grass are real. They are not of my making. They are separate from my Crazy.

Countries aren't real. Governments aren't real. Money isn't real. AK-47s aren't real, but they'll kill you deader than shit. My Crazy isn't real. It is I and countless before me that have given it purchase.

Is love real? Or is it only a real chemical reaction in my blown-up brain?

Is time real? The only meaning I find in the race is the surety of its unpredictable conclusion.

Is the Brotherhood real? What if it feels like the mountain, like it exists outside of me, separate from any one of us? If it is beyond me and the brothers who keep it? If it continues after death? If it endures even after the object of affection is gone?

What if I want the Brotherhood to be real?

What if I need the Brotherhood to be real?

Tadasana. Mountain Pose. Breathe.

"Psycho 7, EOD 6. Stop the convoy," I called over the radio.

"EOD 6, Psycho 7. What's wrong? Why do we need to stop? Over."

"Psycho 7, EOD 6. I can't take it anymore. I need to get one of those watermelons."

"EOD 6, what are you talking about?"

"Psycho 7—just halt and stop traffic for me, okay? We're in a fine neighborhood. I'll just be a minute." I put the radio down.

Through the front windshield of our Humvee I could see the security truck ahead of us slow and stop. Keener pulled in behind him, parked, and turned around to look at me.

"I can't believe you're doing this," he said.

"We've been passing those watermelon stands every day for weeks. It's driving me nuts. Tell me they don't look better than anything in the chow hall," I said.

Keener stayed silent as I checked my gear and got ready to dismount. I picked up my rifle, considered, and put it back down. It would just get in the way.

"I'll be right back. Just give me a minute," I said, and opened the door.

The tumult of downtown Kirkuk hit me in a hot rush as I got out of the armored truck and stepped onto the road. The front and rear security trucks had parked sideways in the center of the road to block traffic, and a line of taxicabs and white sedans were already backing up on this main north-south thoroughfare that cut through the heart of the city. Cars honked their horns, the crowds on the sidewalks stared, and one fruit stand owner looked wide-eyed as I jogged across four lanes of now empty roadway toward his pile of fresh watermelons.

In this Kurdish neighborhood in northern Kirkuk, the main trunk road attracted impromptu markets that sprouted up randomly and varied daily. Men with five-gallon jugs of gasoline and hand pumps. Carts of secondhand electronics and pirated DVDs. And to my envy, wagonloads of fresh fruit grown in the fields and orchards just outside of the city. There is nothing better than a thick, wet, dripping slice of watermelon on a hot day, and Iraq was full of those.

I put up my right hand in a greeting as I approached the fruit seller. He was shorter than I, squat, balding, and with an enormous bushy moustache that covered his entire upper lip. He eyed me nervously until I pointed at his stack of watermelons, put two fingers in the air, and pulled out my wallet.

"How much for two watermelons?" I asked.

He looked in my wallet, and then up at me.

"Two watermelons?" he said in highly accented but passable English. "Two watermelons? Ten dollars. American dollars."

My jaw dropped in surprise. Are you kidding me, I thought. This is highway robbery. Watermelons are a buck or two each back home. Shouldn't they be cheaper here?

"No no no," I said. "No more than two dollars."

The fruit seller smiled at me and laughed.

"Eight dollars," he said. "Two watermelons, eight dollars!"

I started to attract a crowd; the seller's teenage son approached, as well as an eight-year-old boy, a nephew perhaps, who simply stared at me and grinned from ear to ear. Behind me the honking continued, and Castleman ran up and tapped me on the shoulder.

"You ready to go yet? They can't hold traffic forever," he said.

"He wants to haggle, just give me a second," I said to Castleman, and turned back to the amused seller.

I checked my wallet. I had a five and a twenty, and he wasn't getting the twenty.

"Five dollars for two," I said. "My last offer."

"Done!" he cried, clearly pleased, and gathered up in his short arms the two biggest watermelons he had on the stand.

I paid and thanked him, tucked one watermelon under each arm, and jogged with Castleman back to our awaiting convoy. The watermelons were warm from sitting in the sun and fragrant, filling my nose with the memory of splashing through a backyard sprinkler on a summer day. I ran up to the closest security truck and tossed the larger of the two melons up to the gunner manning the .50-cal in the Humvee's turret. He shook his head and laughed as he caught it.

"Split that among the guys when we get back to the FOB," I called as I ran back to my own Humvee where Keener waited impatiently.

That evening, in our private compound, after all the teams were back from missions and the robots were charged and gear cleaned and put away and the sun had set, leaving a dull orange sky, Ewbank cleaned his enormous KA-BAR combat knife at the picnic table just outside the HAS. We had gathered on our front porch, some smoking, all relaxing on a warm desert night, enjoying the cooling air and the accumulated day's heat radiating up off the surrounding concrete.

"Hey Griffin," I called. "Go grab that Tuborg the Special Forces guys dropped off last week." He didn't need to be asked twice, and soon caps popped and bottles clinked, as Ewbank carefully sliced our prize watermelon into fat, juicy wedges. The flesh was the deepest, darkest red I had ever seen, and after one bite we all scrambled like young boys to get seconds. Crisp was the first to spit his seeds at an unwilling victim, his teammate Mitchell, who then chased him around the yard to the amusement of all but Mitchell himself. The inevitable seed-spitting competition began in earnest after that, the participants standing on the concrete benches along the blast wall to gain maximum height advantage. I've forgotten who won. I sipped my beer, and put my feet up, and laughed as the juice of the watermelon dripped down my chin.

"I don't care if they do use human shit as fertilizer," Ewbank said from across the picnic table. "This is the best goddamn watermelon I've ever had."

And it was.

The mountain is real. And the mountain doesn't care if I'm Crazy.

The mountain doesn't concern itself with other mountains

that lie to its left or to its right, or with the valley that lies on the other side, or the glen and wood and swamp beyond. It doesn't care about the future because of the certainty of its present. It cares nothing for the worries or fears or bloodlust I bring to its slopes. It stands alone, a magnificent rise, outside of my head, outside of my Crazy: objective, peaceful, and real.

"Begin your flow. Begin your *vinyasa*," says the Yogini.

Tadasana. Uttanasana. Chaturanga Dandasana. Urdhva Mukha Svanasana. Adho Mukha Svanasana. Tadasana.

Mountain. Standing Forward Bend. Plank and lower. Upward Dog. Downward Dog. Feet forward. Mountain. Repeat your *vinyasa*.

Mountain pose.

The mountain doesn't care if I do or not, if I approach or not, if I am or not, just as it doesn't care what Crazy I bring to it. The slopes are just as steep, the ice just as cold, the winds just as vicious, whether I stand on them or not, whether I stand there Crazy or at peace.

The mountain doesn't care. But the mountain is real. The mountain exists. And the mystery of its objective existence drowns my Crazy.

Why run the race? Because of the amazement that there is a race to be run at all.

"No matter how fast I run, it's never going to be fast enough," I tell my New Shrink.

"Do you enjoy what you are doing? How you are living your life?" she asks.

"Of course not. The Crazy poisons everything," I say.

"Well, start over again," my New Shrink says. "Forget everything you think you need to do. Forget what you almost did. What do you want to do?"

"I want to love my wife, and I want to climb the mountain," I respond.

"Then why don't you?" she says.

I walk outside of the HAS, into the deepest dark night, and feel the first drop on my hand. Then another. And a third. I look up, but the overcast sky has dropped a smothering enveloping blanket and I see nothing. Several more hit my face intermittently, then faster. First, a drizzle. With so much dust in the air, the first drops are more mud than water. Then a shower finally takes hold. The first rain in four months.

"We conclude our yoga practice by breathing the word 'Om,'" my Yogini says. "When you say your Om, pull it from the deepest part of you. Your Om comes from there, up through your body, through your lungs and out of your mouth.

"Send your Om into the universe," says the Yogini. "Your Om will join and harmonize with all that is. Then let it go."

The Om Is and the Om Was.

I stand in the rain, in the real, and prepare my Om.

"You don't have PTSD," my New Shrink says.

"What are you talking about?" I am incredulous.

She turns at her desk, and reaches for a fat book on a nearby shelf. My stomach drops, fills with a nervous hole that briefly overwhelms the Crazy. My New Shrink flips through her clinical handbook, searching for the correct page.

"You don't have nightmares," she starts, scrolling down the list.

No, I dream during the day.

"You don't have one incident, one trauma, that you constantly obsess over, or replay in your mind," she says.

No, there are many.

"You haven't blocked out memories of any trauma," she says.

No, the war is vivid. It's other things that I have forgotten.

"You don't startle at loud noises, or get nervous in public, or avoid places that remind you of what's happened."

Of course not, that passed long ago, and my rifle is ready when I need it.

"You got out of bed this morning. You haven't retreated into a shell and turned off your interaction with the world," she concludes.

Don't be scared of the soft sand.

"But what about the hopelessness . . . and the numbness?" I say. "What about the airport, and the chest pain, and the eye twitches? What about the hairy spider that crawled out of my head?"

What about the bodies and the smells? What about knowing I won't live past today? What about the things I was willing to do? What about my lost faith and innocence?

"What about the Crazy feeling?" I ask. This all can't be for nothing.

"Just because you feel all those things doesn't mean you have PTSD," she chides gently.

"So if I'm not Crazy, then what's wrong with me?"

She laughs a silver waterfall of ringing bells.

"You're human," she says.

I send my Om out into the universe, out of my chest, out of my Crazy, out through my mouth and nose and eyes and cheeks.

A vibration, a sound, a message, a messenger, a traveler, a destination. I send my Om past Ricky's head and Kermit's lake. I send it past Jessie, my wife, past her pain and abandonment and forgotten trials. I send it past Jeff on his boat, past the foot in the box, past the screaming women, past the children and the crowds and through the soft sand. It intermingles with burning cars and exploding robots and the smell of rotting and cooking organs. I send it through the grime and the dust, through the armor and the loneliness. It mixes with my children's smiles and my brothers' love. It gathers all fear and isolation and confusion to itself. My Om passes into oblivion. It dips into the river. It is a cool breeze off the alpine glacier.

The Om Is and the Om Was. It returns from the universe, with the universe, with the pain and the hope and the blood and the helicopters and the artillery rounds falling on Habbaniyah. It returns with my rifle and vest and the Hill of Woe. It returns with driven insight and unwanted knowledge. It returns with the Crazy. It reenters my chakras and fills me full again. It brings the mountain to my feet. Ricky sits to my right. The line of my grandfathers sits to my left.

The Om is my Is and my Was. I am my Om.

The next day, I put on my shoes and go for a run.

Acknowledgments

This book was written while running, much of it on the broad avenues of Grand Island, New York: Stony Point, Huth, East and West River Roads, Whitehaven, and Ransom. Thank you to those that ran with me as well, while working on the road in Texas, Washington, and Tennessee: Jimbo, Bill, Chris, and Schmatt.

In the initial hardcover release, I also thanked these good people, for their influence along the way. Jaime Herbeck, for encouragement that got the ball rolling. Ben Hoffman, for being my first and best reader. Matteah Reppart, for constant love and unconditional support. LaDeane Palmar, for bravely and honestly sharing her story. Ryan Bowers, Ethan Cox, and Josh Tyler, for diligence and thoughtful feedback. Dave Pinkham, for timely input. The writer Stephen Phillips, for providing the big break. My four sons, Virgil, Martin, Samuel, and Elijah, for understanding while Daddy was locked away with the computer in the side room. My agent, Bob Mecoy, for all the little things agents do. And my editor, Gerry Howard, for masterfully helping me craft a better book.

But it turns out that before you publish your first book,

you really have no idea how many souls are going to labor on your behalf, and they deserve my public (though unfortunately belated) thanks as well. First, to my publicist Alison Rich, who continued to schedule interviews and events well beyond quitting time. To Hannah Wood, Kathryn Santora, Joe Gallagher, and John Pitts at Doubleday, who worked all sorts of social media, editorial, and marketing magic. To Dan Zitt, my producer at Random House Audio, who trusted me to read the audiobook (a personal dream fulfilled), and to Scott Sheratt, my director, who helped me make the recording something worth listening to. To Jon Welch, proprietor of Talking Leaves, my local independent bookstore in Buffalo, for hand-selling to anyone who would listen. To my local circle of writers, Mick Cochrane and Matt Higgins, who provide professional sanity and perspective. To the engineers and staff at WBFO, Buffalo's NPR affiliate, who allowed me to take up semi-permanent residency in their studios to do live and taped interviews. And finally and most importantly, my wife, Jessie, whose support didn't stop when the writing was done and has been my touchstone every day since.

Let me end by noting that throughout the writing and publication process of this book, my thoughts have never left the EOD brothers we have lost since the war began. When I started writing, in the summer of 2010, that too-large number was eighty. As of this writing, Christmas of 2012, it is one hundred and twenty-two..